PRAISE FOR

SURVIVOR

. . .

"Claire Culwell is living, breathing proof that each and every preborn life is sacred. Not only does she have a powerful story to share about surviving an abortion attempt, but she also exemplifies Christlike compassion and forgiveness for women who have sought abortions—including her own biological mother. This inspiring book has the potential to change hearts and touch lives!"

—JIM DALY, president of Focus on the Family

"Claire's life, and almost lack thereof, is one full of shocking revelations that are certainly worth telling—but that doesn't mean it's an easy story to share. She does us all a great privilege by sharing the raw, vulnerable, and deepest parts of her life, bringing light to darkness and a lens of mercy to our nation's most divisive topic. Claire's perspective as an abortion-attempt survivor not only tells her own powerful story but also shows how every family member's journey is intricately woven together to reveal God's great love and plan for us."

—CATHERINE HADRO, host and managing editor of EWTN's *Pro-Life Weekly*

"Claire's heart-wrenching and inspiring story is exactly what our world needs today. She bears witness to the beauty and gift of every life, and the transforming power of forgiveness. We would all do well to learn from the story of *Survivor* and let Claire's example convict and encourage us in the fight for life."

—LILA ROSE, president and founder of Live Action and author of *Fighting for Life*

"The beauty of Claire Culwell's story is that it's not just about surviving an abortion; it's about helping others survive too—through unplanned pregnancies, difficult circumstances, and past regrets. While some might have been tempted to let the pain of what happened define them, Claire made a different choice. She allowed God to use her journey to bring a message of hope and healing to a country in desperate need of voices like hers. In a culture that wants us to believe miracles like Claire don't happen, she is living proof: every life has the potential to change the world."

—TONY PERKINS, president of
Family Research Council

SURVIVOR

SURVIVOR

...

An Abortion Survivor's
Surprising Story of
Choosing Forgiveness and
Finding Redemption

CLAIRE CULWELL

with Lois and Steve Rabey

...

FOREWORD BY ABBY JOHNSON

AFTERWORD BY JOSH MCDOWELL

WATERBROOK

Published in the United States by WaterBrook, an imprint of Random House,
a division of Penguin Random House LLC.

WATERBROOK® and its deer colophon are registered trademarks
of Penguin Random House LLC.

Wedding photos by Raquel Davidowitz Photography, copyright © 2020,
www.raqueldphoto.com

All photographs, with the exception of those credited,
are courtesy of the author's personal archives.

LIBRARY OF CONGRESS CATALOGING-IN-PUBLICATION DATA
NAMES: Culwell, Claire, author. | Rabey, Lois Mowday, author. | Rabey, Steve, author.
TITLE: Survivor : an abortion survivor's surprising story of choosing forgiveness and
finding redemption / Claire Culwell, Lois Mowday Rabey, Steve Rabey.
DESCRIPTION: Colorado Springs : WaterBrook, 2021. | Includes bibliographical references.
IDENTIFIERS: LCCN 2020037082 | ISBN 9780593193228 (paperback) |
ISBN 9780593193235 (ebook)
SUBJECTS: LCSH: Abortion—Moral and ethical aspects. | Abortion—Religious aspects—
Christianity. | Pro-life movement.
CLASSIFICATION: LCC HQ767.15 .C784 2021 | DDC 362.1988/8—dc23
LC record available at https://lccn.loc.gov/2020037082

Printed in the United States of America on acid-free paper

waterbrookmultnomah.com

2 4 6 8 9 7 5 3 1

First Edition

SPECIAL SALES Most WaterBrook books are available at special quantity discounts when
purchased in bulk by corporations, organizations, and special-interest groups. Custom
imprinting or excerpting can also be done to fit special needs. For information, please email
specialmarketscms@penguinrandomhouse.com.

I lovingly dedicate this book to

my mom and dad,

my sister, Rachel,

my husband, David,

my precious children,

and my birth mother.

This is our story, and I am honored

to be able to share it.

FOREWORD

. . .

As an abortion clinic director, I believed many things to be true. I believed abortions empowered women. I believed women had a right to abortion. I believed abortion was health care. I also believed many things to be untrue. I did not believe the pro-lifers who said that some women regretted their abortions. I did not believe them when they said that women could suffer long-term physical and emotional damage from abortion.

And there was one thing that I had never considered. I had never considered that a baby could actually survive an abortion procedure.

I remember the day I met Claire. My life had just been turned upside down because of my simple decision to quit my position at Planned Parenthood. I had been with the abortion giant for eight years and abruptly resigned from my position as clinic director after witnessing a live abortion procedure on an ultrasound monitor. I wasn't supposed to see what I saw. This tiny yet perfectly formed baby wasn't supposed to feel the suction tube as it entered the home that had been his place of safety for thirteen weeks. But when the tube touched his body, he jumped. He jumped as if he had been disturbed from a peaceful sleep. And when the powerful suction was turned on, I watched a gruesome tug-of-war begin. This baby was fighting so hard, moving his arms and legs, but the suction was simply too powerful. In just a matter of moments, the screen was black. The womb was empty. The jar was full. My life had been changed.

I left my job quietly, never planning to speak publicly about what I had seen. I sought help from the Coalition for Life, a local pro-life group who had been praying for me for all those years. They had always promised to help me find another job if I ever decided to walk away. But it had become more than that. It wasn't just about a job anymore. I had experienced a conversion. My heart of stone had become a heart of flesh. Christ had changed me and made me a new creation. I needed a new start, and I found that with my new friends at the Coalition for Life. I didn't want to speak. I wanted to slink away quietly and heal privately.

God had other plans. Several weeks later, I found myself in a court battle with Planned Parenthood, which then turned into a media firestorm I could never have imagined. After all, why would Planned Parenthood attempt to silence one of their directors? What do they have to hide? These were the questions I was being asked by all the major media networks across the world. I was overwhelmed by this new life, these new friends, these phone lines that would never stop ringing with reporters on the other end wanting to ask me questions that I didn't know how to answer.

And in the midst of this chaos, a quiet young woman walked into the Coalition for Life office with a piece of paper in her hand. She was greeted by one of the staff members, and I remember them asking, "Do you want to meet Abby Johnson?" In a sort of confused voice, Claire responded, "Um, yeah, okay." I could tell she had no idea who I was. She hadn't seen the breaking news story on the local ten o'clock news program. She probably didn't follow the Drudge Report. I was no celebrity to her. *Thank goodness,* I thought. She handed me the piece of paper that was in her hand. "I just wanted to drop off my story. I recently found out that I'm an abortion survivor, and I want to see if maybe I could use my story to help women choose life."

An abortion survivor? I had no idea what that meant. Was that a joke? People don't survive abortions. That's the whole point of an abortion. Death. Destruction. Yet here was this beautiful woman standing in front of me, so I knew I must have misunderstood. "What do you mean?" I asked.

She went on to tell me her story. We didn't sit down to chat about the explosive details she had found out about her life from the birth mother she had met only months before. We just stood in the middle of the reception area, a living room of an old house that had been converted into an office. No one was paying attention to us anyway. The staff from the Coalition for Life was scurrying around, answering the ringing phones, managing the unending stacks of messages from reporters that I needed to call back about interviews, and visiting with the local reporters and supporters who were coming by for a quick word. Yet here we stood, everyone around us unaware of the profound moment that was taking place: a former abortion clinic director standing face to face with a woman who had been saved from an abortion. A young woman standing face to face with a woman who had participated in the act that had almost taken her life many years ago. I was, for the first time, facing the humanity that existed in the womb—humanity that I had helped destroy more than twenty-two thousand times. While we stood in that truth, a lifelong friendship began.

Under all normal circumstances, Claire and I should not be friends. In her flesh, Claire should feel anger when she looks at me. Her neck should get red and hot when she hears my name. She should be disgusted when she thinks of me. People like me are the reason she is without her twin sibling. People like me are the reason she almost lost her life. In my flesh, I shouldn't be able to look Claire in the eye. I should be ashamed to even be in her presence. I should run the other direction every time I see her coming my way.

But *God*. God makes our friendship make sense. God makes it so a former abortion clinic director and an abortion survivor can be best friends. Only God can do that. Only God can turn anger into forgiveness. Only God can turn shame into mercy. God makes a way for new beginnings, and he made a way for me and Claire. We have lived this journey together for more than ten years. We have hurt together, healed together, cheered for each other, had babies, worked hard, played harder, loved well, been mad at each other, made up and laughed about it, taken care of each other after surgery, traveled together. We have been able to live life together because Claire was able to *live*. The chance to live is something most of us take for granted, yet it has resulted in incredible complexities for Claire.

You will love Claire's story. As you read, you will feel heartbroken. You will celebrate victories. You will absolutely fall in love with Claire and her sweet spirit. But more than anything, you will marvel at God. You will see his goodness displayed in the lives of his children. You will be blessed.

I will meditate on the glorious splendor of Your majesty,
And on Your wondrous works.
Men shall speak of the might of Your awesome acts,
And I will declare Your greatness.
They shall utter the memory of Your great goodness,
And shall sing of Your righteousness.

PSALM 145:5–7, NKJV

—Abby Johnson, bestselling author
of *Unplanned* and former
Planned Parenthood clinic director

PREFACE

. . .

THE SECRET THAT TURNED ME
UPSIDE DOWN

SHE SAT ON THE BED NEXT TO ME, SOBBING AND SHAKING. The look of anguish in her eyes told me that something terrible was about to be revealed.

My birth mother stammered through the truth about my birth. It was not the story I had believed for the past twenty years. I put my arm around her as the shock pulsed through my mind. In a moment, the story of who I was changed radically. At once, I saw that just about everything I had assumed about my birth was not what had happened at all.

I knew I had been adopted, but because my adoptive parents were so loving and kind, I never experienced the gnawing hunger that makes some adoptees feel they need to uncover all the facts of their birth.

So far I had been more than content with my life. I had been blessed by parents who claimed they loved me more than anyone had ever loved a child and who backed up that bold claim through their loving actions, moment by moment and day by day.

Most of the details surrounding my birth mother's pregnancy and her decision to place me for adoption were unknown to my parents because my adoption was closed. It seemed that, for the rest of my life, important information about who I was and how I got here was destined to remain walled off from me in some dusty archive.

But then my younger sister, Rachel, upset this delicate balance. Two years after they adopted me, my parents welcomed Rachel in an open adoption after a young woman they had known for years faced an unplanned pregnancy.

When Rachel was a teenager, she met her birth mother and established positive ongoing contact with her. The more I learned about this experience, the more my desire to do the same with my birth mother grew. At that point, all I knew about my origins—and all I really needed to know—could be summarized in two simple truths: my birth mother had unexpectedly become pregnant with me when she was thirteen; she had chosen to give me life and place me for adoption.

But as she tearfully confessed to me that day, only one of those statements was true. She *hadn't* chosen to give birth to me. Instead, at the insistence of her own mother, she underwent an abortion to take care of the "problem" that was me.

Problem solved, or so she and her mother thought. Weeks later, my birth mother realized that somehow she was still pregnant. I had survived. And since by then she was in her third trimester, it was too late for a legal abortion in her home state of Oklahoma. Her mother could not accept this surprising predicament and forced her to go to Kansas, where third-trimester abortions were legal.

I might have been subjected to another abortion attempt if not for an injury my birth mother had sustained during her first abortion. The amniotic sac that was holding me had been ripped and was leaking fluid. If not for this damage, my birth mother likely would have undergone a second—and successful—abortion.

That revelation sent my mind, heart, and nervous system into overdrive. Mixed emotions swirled in my head as I sat on the bed that night in 2009. I didn't know what to do with how I felt. I couldn't even sort out what I did feel—confusion, sadness, anger, fear. My birth mother left the room, and I sat there and stared at the wall. The shock of what I had just heard paralyzed me.

Finally I lifted my head and cried out in a silent prayer, *What do I do now? What do you want me to do?*

I didn't get an answer that night to my question, but I got an assurance that has proved true through the journey that has followed. God promised that he would be with me every step of the way as I worked through the process of absorbing the knowledge that my birth mother and grandmother had tried to end my life before I left the womb. I'd been completely unwanted.

It's hard to explain how I knew that God would be with me, but I have always sensed that during difficult moments in my life. My parents taught me that trusting in Jesus meant that I could ask him for help and that he would give it to me. I've carried that teaching with me all through my life. So, when I asked God those questions, I also prayed, *Please be with me no matter what this all means.* I felt peace that God's presence would give me whatever I needed to move forward.

I had survived an attempt on my life. And looking back, I can see how my life had been preserved, nurtured, and guided and how God's plan for my life had been unfolding all along. I didn't know it then, but there was a purpose in my receiving this surprising information.

After finding out I'd survived an abortion, I developed an interest in pro-life issues. And in time, that interest grew and grew. Soon I began telling my story to small groups at schools and churches near me—a major accomplishment for one of the world's quietest introverts. And eventually, telling my life story would become my calling.

I talk about the joys of adoption and the sorrows of abortion, but I always stress that women like my birth mother—women who unexpectedly face major life-and-death decisions—don't need lectures or chants of "Baby Killer." They need God's forgiveness and grace to heal and recover from their grief.

In the following pages, you will read a survivor's story—my story—filled with grace and redemption. The parents who adopted me provided a safe and healing home that gave me a foundation to follow God's leading to where I am today. I remain close to my parents and have a loving relationship with my birth mother. I am married and have a beautiful family. God has made clear to me what my calling is and has opened doors for me to fulfill that calling.

You may be reading this and thinking, *I don't have any of those wonderful things in my life. How can I relate to this woman who has so much?*

I can assure you, I have struggled—and still do—with pain and difficulties. My life has had many ups and downs. There are still questions I grapple with. And as you read my story, you'll see that the older I get, the more complicated my life becomes.

You may be an adoptee, a woman who has had an abortion, or a woman who is considering an abortion. You may be pregnant and deciding whether to place your baby for adoption or raise your baby yourself. You may be a man who has fathered a baby in an unplanned pregnancy. You may be the parent or the friend of a person who fits one of these descriptions. You may even be a prochoice activist who has secretly picked up this book. Or you may be a reader who simply questions how to sort out the controversy over abortion.

No matter who you are or where you find yourself, I hope my story will encourage and inspire you. Most of all, I hope you will see that the grace and redemption in my story can be your story too.

—Claire Culwell

CONTENTS

...

SURVIVOR

PART ONE

. . .

Wanted, Chosen,
Loved

1.

CHOSEN, LOVED, ADOPTED

. . .

"SO, CLAIRE, ARE YOU REALLY ADOPTED?"

"That's weird."

"What's that like?"

"Did you live in an orphanage?"

"I'm sorry you're adopted."

My elementary school friends weren't trying to be rude or mean. Most were merely curious. But their occasional questions surprised me.

"Yeah, and what was it like living in an orphanage?"

Most of us kids had seen the movie *Annie*, which was based on the old comic strip *Little Orphan Annie*. Annie lived in a big New York orphanage run by a mean alcoholic woman who made all the children work and clean every day. Annie tried to escape but was caught and returned to the orphanage, where she was later adopted by a wealthy man named Oliver Warbucks.

"I've never seen an orphanage," I told my friends, "and being adopted is wonderful."

My parents had actually convinced me that adopting was the

preferred way to create a family. While most mommies and daddies simply accepted the babies that were born to them, my mommy and daddy searched and searched until they found me—the perfect baby for them.

Then, once they took me home, they loved me with all their hearts.

"We loved you more than anybody has ever loved a baby," Daddy always told me. I'm pretty sure almost all parents feel that way about their children, but my sister and I always felt affirmed when our parent repeated those words.

I tried to explain it all to my friends.

"My mom and dad wanted me. They chose me. They love me," I said. "And it's not like being adopted makes me any different than you."

In time, I would learn much more about Warren and Barbara Culwell—when they met, how they fell in love, and how they faced difficult struggles to create our wonderful family.

In fact, I often heard them tell their story when college students and other guests who had gathered around our big dinner table asked them how they got together.

It was December 1979, and Warren Culwell was in Atlanta to attend the annual Christmas conference of Campus Crusade for Christ—now named Cru—the ministry that works with students and others all over the world.

After two years on Crusade's campus staff at Ole Miss, Warren was given a plum assignment: serving as personal assistant to Josh McDowell, the ministry's globe-trotting superstar speaker.

McDowell was able to transform Christian apologetics from an abstract academic exercise into compelling talks he delivered to millions of young people. He wrote *Evidence That Demands a Ver-*

dict, a classic that has sold more than one million copies and is still in print.

Many young people rejected Christianity during the turbulence of the 1960s and 1970s, but McDowell assured his audiences that having faith in a resurrected Christ and trusting in the Bible's teaching were not only intellectually defensible but also the only way to live. Warren traveled with McDowell from city to city, handling logistics and working with local Crusade staff to follow up with the many students who had come to faith through the events.

Barbara Griffes, a college senior, was four years younger than Warren. She had come to Crusade's Christmas conference to learn, grow her faith, and apply for a job. Faith in Christ was central to her life, and she wanted to join Crusade so she could share the gospel message with young people desperately searching for answers to life's challenges.

Barbara was riding up an escalator when Warren spotted the attractive newcomer from the floor above. Something about her caught his eye. As she got closer, he could make out her name tag. But instead of quietly introducing himself when she got off the escalator, Warren, who could be energetic, joyful, outgoing, and a bit irreverent, called out to her in a voice that others nearby could hear.

"Barbara, I love you!" he shouted.

Startled and a bit embarrassed, Barbara smiled and walked on by. But it wasn't the last time these two would cross paths.

They met again—but only briefly—in February 1980. Warren had traveled with Josh McDowell to a speaking engagement at Auburn University, where Barbara was a student leader. They talked, but then Warren was quickly on the road again.

That summer, they would finally have some time to get to know each other better. Both were taking training classes at Crusade's Institute of Biblical Studies in Colorado when one of Warren's friends suggested a double date with Barbara and one of her friends. The two couples spent a beautiful day at Elitch Gardens, an amusement park in Denver.

By the end of the day, my mom-and-dad-to-be had grown more serious about each other.

In the gathering twilight, the two of them were strapped into a little car on a big Ferris wheel. As they sat close together, their car rotated up to the top and paused, giving them a stunning view of Denver's city lights and the vast expanse of the Rocky Mountains to the west.

That was the moment Warren looked at Barbara and thought, *You know, this is the kind of girl I want to spend the rest of my life with.*

Things moved quickly after that. Between Crusade classes on the Bible and theology, the two sought each other out during campfires and horse rides in the Rocky Mountains. As they talked about their lives, shared their favorite Bible verses, and discussed their passion for ministry, their affection grew.

"Each of us knew we wanted to share our lives with someone who was devoted to serving Christ," my mom explained to me.

And in June 1981—a year and a half after they met—they were married.

But married life turned out to be even busier than they expected. Their first years of marriage were hectic.

Mom was on staff with Crusade at Southern Methodist University in Dallas, leading Bible studies for sorority girls and other students while also discipling young people who were interested in experiencing a deeper relationship with Christ.

Dad worked with male students at SMU while attending Dallas Theological Seminary.

Both believed the work they were doing with students was vital, so they gave 110 percent of their time and energy to ministry. They assumed they would have kids and start a family at some point, as both came from big, loving families. But they had no idea when they would get around to it. Life was full, the demands of ministry were never ending, and they were in no hurry.

Then came Hawaii.

In 1984, Crusade dispatched them to a distant tropical paradise for a summer assignment: teaching forty college students how to grow in their Christian faith and share it naturally with others on their campuses.

Their lodging was far from romantic. They stayed at the Hawaii School for Girls, where they slept on cots. But the setting—near Diamond Head, a gorgeous volcanic crater—was beautiful and inspired thoughts of a family. They were ready.

"God," they prayed aloud together, "please bless us and give us a beautiful baby!"

Dad prayed more specifically: for a beautiful baby boy who would carry on his family name.

A short time later, Mom didn't feel well, which got her excited. *Is this my first bout of morning sickness?* she wondered.

No. She was not pregnant but merely taking the first steps of a long journey of waiting, wondering, believing, and doubting.

People deal with challenges in different ways, and my mom and dad faced infertility in dramatically different ways.

Dad's default approach is to be hopeful and positive about the future. He's a visionary who always looks ahead to what God can do tomorrow. His approach to their inability to conceive was optimistic. "If our plan A doesn't work out, God will have an even better plan B for us."

But Mom's barren years were difficult for her as she struggled to understand why God was not choosing to give them the baby they had hoped and prayed for.

She often compared herself with her Crusade friends, many of whom seemed blessed with supernatural fertility, according to their frequent, joyful announcements of their pregnancies.

"I went to baby shower after baby shower and always hoped I'd have one myself," she once told me. She described this period of her life as "living in a waiting room."

Mom discussed some of these trials and tribulations in the regular newsletter that she and Dad sent to friends and supporters of their work with Crusade. The May 1987 newsletter was headlined "Wait Wait Wait . . ."

While she gave her supporters a general sense of her frustration with waiting, my mom poured out her heart more fully in her journals, which she shared with me. The one from 1985 was tinged with heartbreak in nearly every entry.

> What if we can't ever have any children?
> I guess God is still in control. That's a lot to
> think about. But I'm not going to worry
> about it. I hope.
>
> We went to the Dr. again. . . . We need to go
> back again next month. Again. I know your
> intentions toward me are for good.
>
> We got a letter from the Dr. that doesn't sound
> very good at all. They are going to do one more
> test. I guess God is still in control. It's hard to
> think I might never be pregnant. I know

everyone always "wants something." It keeps
us trusting the Lord, I guess.

She tried to stay focused on serving others, but that didn't always calm her disappointments:

Lord, I want to have that confident trust in
you always. I know I haven't suffered to the
point Job has. Right now I feel kind of neutral
about things. No major problems but I'm just
not real fired up about anything either. I hope
this will be a good week with the girls I am
discipling.

One of my friends that has been trying to get
pregnant for 10 years just found out she is
pregnant!! What a miracle!! For some reason
yesterday it made me sort of depressed, though.
Lord, I need you to help me. I feel like
nobody really understands what I feel.

This week has been the hardest of all. Another
one of my friends is pregnant. I cried and
cried. I talked with a student that asked me
how I was doing and cried some more.

When I asked my dad about this time, he acknowledged that he had missed an opportunity to love and care for Mom as she suffered.

"It was a busy time for us. I spent almost every night with students, giving, giving, and giving. I did not pick up on her deep struggle, nor did I enter into her grief over this great loss we were facing together. Years later, when we watched a movie about adoption, we wept together over the couple not able to have a baby naturally. I wished I could have listened and cared for and cried with Barbara as she waited and wrestled."

Mom and Dad tried to keep hope alive as the waiting and wrestling continued. They did more than pray about their infertility. They spent years setting up difficult meetings with a series of infertility specialists, trying a variety of treatments, including intrauterine insemination, without success.

One doctor was particularly blunt: "I think you have a 1 percent chance of ever conceiving a child, and I'm being generous with the 1 percent because of God," he said. He gave them a list of twenty-four adoption agencies.

Mom was devastated when the door finally shut on her hopes of having a baby. She experienced the only real crisis of faith she's ever known. As she wrote in her journal,

> I believed in my heart that God was good, and that his plans for us were good. But I felt like my prayers and concerns didn't really matter to him. My mind and my heart were at odds with one another. I wondered, Does God really care about me and my desire to have a baby? Has he forgotten all about me?

Even though giving birth to their own baby had been their plan A, they soon embraced God's plan B. As Mom started calling the twenty-four adoption agencies on the list, the waiting entered a new phase. There would be two years of filling out forms, taking training classes, and waiting for that special call from an agency before I arrived on the scene.

At one point, they thought they were approved to adopt, only to be told by a social worker that they were not yet ready because they hadn't sufficiently grieved over their infertility. It was frustrating, but as they waited, they knew God was orchestrating the timing and finding just the right baby for them.

They spent months meeting in discussion groups with other couples who were working through their sorrow and anger over being infertile. Then suddenly, after years of waiting, things started happening.

A social worker notified them they were approved to adopt, which made Mom feel like she had become pregnant at last.

Finally they got *the call*.

The social worker explained that a baby (me) had been born prematurely to a fourteen-year-old Oklahoma mother. I weighed just over three pounds and, as is often the case with premature births, had complications. But it would be years before we understood why.

"Do you want this baby girl?" the social worker asked.

Mom and Dad would need to sleep on it before deciding.

They took the next few days to think it over and consider the complications. My birth had been rough. I was born with clubfeet and a dislocated hip that would require me to spend the first two months of my life in the hospital. Dad wondered whether they would be able to afford the years of medical bills, therapy, and surgery that might be required to make my body whole.

Plus, I was a girl, not the boy Dad had originally imagined. As a card-carrying resident of the Lone Star State who had been taught by his dad to hunt and fish in the piney woods of East Texas, Dad had always dreamed of teaching his son to hunt and fish. He also wanted to pass on his family name to a son because, without a male child, this Culwell family line would end with him.

But, during the months and months of waiting, Dad grew to love the idea of being a dad to a little girl. He thanked God for this precious new life and was eager to hold their baby girl in his arms. After a few frantic calls to their health insurance company to make sure my care would be covered, Mom and Dad were gung ho to go.

"Yes," they told the agency. "We would love to take her."

They decided they would name me Lauren Claire. *Lauren* means "victorious one," which was perfect, since by the time I was a few months old, I had already been victorious so many times.

The night before they were to come to the hospital and see me for the first time, each one of them wrote a letter to my teenage birth mother, in care of the adoption agency. Mom had got this idea from one of the many books she read during her years of waiting. It was called *Dear Birth Mother: Thank You for Our Baby.*[1]

They didn't know my birth mother's name, so Dad addressed his letter to "Dear Special Friend," telling her, "I've been waiting to write to you for two months and tell you how I prayed for you and your baby girl."

And they both prayed, asking God to make it possible for them to meet my birth mother someday.

The timing of my arrival proved perfect. Four days after my parents took me home from the hospital, they got to take me to church on Mother's Day. Mom couldn't believe she was finally a mama! Her years of waiting and wrestling were over. She always says she's sure she was the happiest mother that Mother's Day.

2.

A HAPPY BABY

. . .

I'M TOLD I WAS A VERY HAPPY BABY. I DIDN'T CRY MUCH and had a sweet disposition. That's somewhat surprising, considering my challenging circumstances. After my parents took me home, I continued to deal with the many medical problems I had faced since my birth.

The January before my first birthday, my parents began preparing me for hip surgery by placing me in traction for hours at a time with weights and pulleys working against my muscles to straighten my body.

I must have looked pretty strange all tangled up in the creative devices my parents and doctors contrived to keep most of my body mobile while securing my legs in the needed upraised position. They attached a pulley and a rope to my little red wagon and hooked it up to me, holding my legs in the air. I don't remember it, but I'm sure it was an awkward position to be in for two long weeks.

During that time, God blessed us with a neighbor who would become my pediatric orthopedic surgeon. He was kind enough to stop by our house and gently work with my legs to help prepare them for surgery. Mom would be close by, smiling at his generosity as she watched him speak softly to me while moving my legs.

I don't know whether he would have done that if we hadn't been neighbors. But he took time out of his professional life to walk over to our house and work with me to help ensure a successful surgery. Success meant that I would be able to walk one day. My parents were hopeful, but the thought of their infant going through any kind of operation must have created some anxiety.

On the day of my surgery, I was wheeled into an operating room and put under anesthesia. The surgeon began to maneuver my legs much like he did when he had come to our house. The nurses and others assisting in the operation were all prepped, waiting for him to place my legs and hip in the correct position.

Then it happened. *Pop!* My hip had popped back into place!

And just like that, no surgery was needed.

I'm sure the surgeon was almost as excited as my parents when he gave them the good news. He burst into the waiting room and told them that I would not need surgery after all.

They couldn't wait for me to come out of the anesthesia. It wasn't long before the recovery room nurse led my eager parents to my bed.

"Claire!" Dad hollered. "Claire, you don't need surgery after all. You're going to be just fine!" Of course, I don't remember any of it, but my dad always tells this story with the same enthusiasm he felt that day.

Even with traction behind me, I had multiple foot and body casts ahead of me. Anyone who's ever worn a cast knows that after a while they can start to smell pretty disgusting. That's true even when making valiant attempts to keep everything spotlessly clean.

Imagine how the stench would increase if diarrhea permeated the cast! Well, that's what happened to me. I had picked up a stomach bug, and the resulting diarrhea seeped into my body cast. The doctors wouldn't allow the cast to be changed, so my mom did her best to clean me up. Total success was impossible, but her efforts made it possible for us all to endure. Eventually the diarrhea stopped, the cast was taken off, and I was finally free to walk just like any other toddler ready to explore her world.

Mom and Dad took on a challenge when they chose me, and they willingly took good care of me every step of the way. I never heard them complain once about any of the struggles my health problems posed. In fact, they've insisted many times that they never thought of my early years as difficult.

Having no previous experience with raising a baby, they simply accepted my needs as part of the package, knowing that all parents face problems. Perhaps their many years of failing to conceive a child helped prepare them to experience pure joy when their dream came true. I wasn't the bouncing baby boy my father had envisioned, but they embraced me and adored me just the same.

I know that adoption doesn't always work out the way it did for me. I was spared the struggles some adoptees face, thanks to a mom and dad who chose me and who loved me with all their hearts. What more could a kid want?

I don't remember Mom and Dad talking to me about adoption early on, but I do remember them trying to explain our family situation like this: "Claire, while you were growing in someone else's tummy, you were growing in both of our hearts at the same time."

That made perfect sense to me. And I would learn much more as I saw the whole adoption process play out before my eyes— when I got my very own baby sister!

3.

OUR FAMILY OF FOUR

. . .

"CLAIRE, WE'VE GOT SOME EXCITING NEWS TO TELL you," my dad said, a big grin on his face. My mom was standing next to him with her own beaming smile. The two of them sat on the living room sofa, and my mom pulled me onto her lap.

"You're going to be getting a new baby sister!" Dad declared.

I was so thrilled that I tumbled over into my dad's lap and just about burst with joy. Or so I am told. I was only two years old and don't really remember the big announcement. But Mom and Dad have often repeated the story of my reaction.

It was all going to happen like my own arrival did. My sister was growing inside someone's tummy somewhere. Mom and Dad had already chosen her as their own. When everything was ready, the three of us would fly out to California and pick her up.

Mom and Dad both hoped and prayed adoption number two would come with fewer complications than number one had. In fact, they assumed everything would be easier the second time around because they already knew the people they'd be working with and understood the hoops they'd need to jump through.

They returned to the same adoption agency, Deaconess Pregnancy & Adoption in Oklahoma City, a Christian organization with a commitment to creating loving families like ours. Their mission was clear—*reflect Christ's redeeming love by transforming the lives of children, empowering women in unplanned pregnancies, creating families through adoption, and supporting all with counseling and guidance throughout their journey*—and my parents felt confident in them. Especially after they so lovingly walked through the adoption process with me.

However, within a week of contacting Deaconess, Mom and Dad received a phone call that surprised them.

A longtime family friend reached out and asked my parents to both get on the phone. She knew they were beginning the process of adopting another child.

"I have a baby for you!" she yelled excitedly.

Then she gave them the details. The woman with the unplanned pregnancy was someone they knew, someone who had seen how my mom and dad loved me. That's why she wanted my parents to be the ones to adopt her baby girl.

This process would be so very different from when they adopted me.

Everything about my birth mother had been a big mystery. My adoption had been closed, meaning they didn't know anything about my birth mother that she didn't want to reveal to them. But this would be an open adoption, in which all parties knew everyone's story. My parents already knew the birth mom, and they were grateful to receive health reports as her pregnancy progressed.

Many adoption experts say an open adoption, when handled appropriately, can be happier and healthier for both the birth mother and the child. But Dad wasn't sure, and he worked out his ambivalence and uncertainty in the pages of his journal:

Yesterday a friend called and said she had a baby for us! Someone we knew. We talked to the mother for two hours on the phone last night. Kind of awkward but good. She seems to be doing okay.

I can't imagine the shame, guilt and feelings she must have. Scary and embarrassing, with her friends. Oh I ache for her and want to cry for her. I know she has gone through a lot. I know her and it causes great pain.

I ask you, Lord, for clear thinking in all of this. She needs you.

My question is, Are we the best for her and this baby? Knowing her, is that a problem?

My mom never entertained such questions. She knew right away that this baby was meant to be with us. She even had a name picked out: Rachel Florence Culwell. Her middle name was to honor Dad's grandmother.

Mom understood Dad's need to take a breath before giving his personal okay, but she was pretty certain that he would say yes.

Dad spent some time taking his questions to the Lord. But it didn't take God long to answer Dad and affirm to him that Rachel was to be a part of our family. He joined Mom in celebrating this wonderful news. They immediately called Deaconess to stop that adoption process and instead began a private adoption with Olivia, Rachel's birth mother.

Olivia lived in California. So my mom and dad arranged to fly up there as soon as they received word that Rachel's birth was near. I got to go with them to bring my precious sister home.

When the day arrived, my parents went to the hospital while I stayed with some family friends. When Mom and Dad got back later that day, they told me that Rachel was a beautiful, healthy baby. I would get to go meet her myself the very next day.

"Stister! Rachel! Rachel! Where are you?" I remember calling out as I rushed down the hall of the hospital for my first meeting with my brand-new baby sister.

I was dressed in my Easter Sunday best. I wore a peach-colored dress with white flowers and a big white collar. My white sandals matched my white hat that sat atop my dark brown curls.

I hadn't been walking on my own for long, so I still wobbled a bit, but I made steady progress down the hall, carrying a gift bag that contained a "Mary Had a Little Lamb" toy and a pacifier. When I arrived in Olivia's room, my dad sat me in a big chair and placed a tightly wound bundle in my arms. I quickly and carefully unraveled the blanket and gazed at my wonderful, precious baby sister.

I had always wished for a real baby as I nurtured and cared for the doll babies that were among my favorite toys. Now the baby in my arms was not a doll but a living, breathing baby who had wrapped her tiny hand around my finger. I didn't want to let her go.

"Can we take her with us now?" I asked.

No, my parents explained. Not yet. But we would come back the next day and take Rachel home with us to Texas.

I was too little to understand it at the time, but I have often thought since about the great courage it took for Olivia to place Rachel with us after giving birth to her.

It's difficult to fathom the courage and love of a birth mother who can set aside her powerful, natural emotions in order to put her child first and make the difficult decision to place her baby in the hands of a family that will love and provide for the child. This is a supreme act of love—the kind of love that only a mother can know.

I could see tears in Olivia's eyes as she handed Rachel to my mom in the hospital room while her family and my parents and I gathered around her hospital bed.

Olivia's dad prayed over Rachel as Olivia gave her to my mom. Our family of four was complete.

MY SISTER, MY FRIEND

Rachel and I were typical siblings growing up, with the usual ups and downs. We would spend days and weeks at a time as the best of friends. Then something would happen to ignite an argument. She'd borrow a top from my closet without asking me. I'd take a CD from her room and loan it to a friend. We'd have words over it; then the offender would apologize and the offended would accept the apology. Those arguments never lasted long, and we'd soon be back to a smooth relationship.

When we were younger, one of the games we loved to play was called "orphanage." We'd dress up and pretend we lived in an orphanage, scrubbing floors and trying to hide from the mean matron. We were strong and brave and always stuck together, and our goal was to escape and go looking for our parents.

Of course, the game was based on our imagination, not our own life story. And after we played, we reveled in the fact that we had loving parents and a home to call our own.

Rachel felt as positive about being adopted as I did. We had wonderful parents who had chosen us and loved us.

I can remember students coming to our home to talk with my parents or to attend Bible studies they taught in the relaxed environment of our family room. Rachel and I got to see firsthand how our parents lived their faith in everyday life.

They felt called to this ministry, and it eventually took us beyond the familiar life we knew in Texas.

COSTA RICA

In 1996, Mom and Dad got an assignment that would require them to relocate to Costa Rica for eight months. We girls knew that our neighbors enjoyed family vacations, but nobody we knew went that far away for that long. Leaving their two beloved daughters behind in the United States would never be Mom and Dad's plan, so Rachel and I would be going with them, even if we weren't enthusiastic about it.

I was scared about what we might face and uncomfortable about leaving my familiar places and friends, and I had no interest in starting first grade in a foreign country.

Plus, once we arrived in Costa Rica, it sure didn't seem like a vacation.

Mom and Dad attended language school to quickly learn Spanish so they could effectively reach Latin American young people. While they were studying Spanish, Rachel and I went to the nearby English-speaking missionary school housed in the same complex.

Once they could speak Spanish, my parents spent their time at the University of Costa Rica, sharing Christ with students and leading Bible studies. In the summer, when school was out, they worked with students from the United States on summer mission teams.

Dad loved teaching young people how to read the Bible, especially the Old Testament, while Mom loved meeting with students and helping them grow in their relationship with the Lord.

The weather was beautiful, our Costa Rica house was nice, and there were other missionary families on our block. The school was about a mile from our home, so we kids walked to and from school together every day. Lush green lawns, flowering hedges, and carved stone pathways made the language school's campus beautiful. The outer walls of the children's school were brightly painted with sea creatures and huge multicolored flowers.

All this should have made me feel happy, but it didn't work out that way. Just a few weeks after we got settled, we learned that my mom's parents were on a cruise that would be stopping in Costa Rica. So our family made plans to meet them when their ship docked in our new country.

We had a wonderful visit. I loved spending time with my grandfather. It didn't matter to me that years before, Gramps had suffered two strokes that left him without the ability to speak and made swallowing difficult. I hadn't known him before the strokes, so our nonverbal communication seemed normal to me.

He expressed his love to me with great hugs, big smiles, and eyes that said "I love you!" His disability didn't disturb me or make me want to distance myself from him. In fact, I wanted to be close to him, to try to meet any need he had. Though we spent just a few days together, being with him brought out my nurturing side as I helped feed him and love on him.

When we took Grammy and Gramps back to the ship for the rest of their cruise, we hugged and talked about seeing them again after our time in Costa Rica. I remember feeling happy and satisfied to have spent time with them. Little did I know that that would be my last visit with Gramps. He died three days later from a chok-ing incident while still on the ship.

I was devastated. I couldn't understand how I could feel happy knowing I wouldn't ever see Gramps again. I wanted to help Gramps, but now there was nothing I could do.

I look back now and believe that I was created with empathy. Gramps was Gramps, whether he could talk or not. People who were handicapped or otherwise different didn't seem off-putting to me. It wasn't something I learned. It was—and is—just who I am.

Mom believes that the shock of losing Gramps after just being with him traumatized me. He had been his usual happy self, and then suddenly he was gone. We all flew back to Seattle for Gramps's burial. The loss, along with the trip and the experience of a funeral, was a lot for me to absorb. I barely had time to adjust before we flew right back to Costa Rica and got ready for school to begin.

I was a different kid after we returned. The loss of Gramps caused me to withdraw into myself, and I wasn't excited about going to a new school in an unfamiliar place.

I don't remember my first day at school, but I remember well how quickly my school days became unbearable. My easygoing personality and nurturing spirit suffered setbacks under a teacher who intimidated me.

My teacher didn't greet me with a smile as I entered her class-room, and she seemed totally unconcerned when I sat shaking in my seat. Her severe manner scared me. I don't think I had ever encountered someone who was so unkind. These feelings were new to me, and I didn't know how to cope with them. I couldn't keep from crying when she addressed me with her stern voice. Tears would fall behind my glasses, and I would bolt out of my seat to seek help in the principal's office.

The principal was a gentle, compassionate, grandpa-type refuge for me. Maybe the loss of Gramps drew me to him and engendered a familiarity that comforted me. I was so introverted and he was so kind.

I would sit in the principal's office for what felt like hours just to calm my nervousness. I remember he used the time to teach me miscellaneous lessons that seemed fun instead of intimidating. One of my favorites was when he'd point out places on a big map and tell me about them.

Still, I hated my classroom and would do everything I could to get out of it. My parents were at a loss about how to help me. Even our walks to school became battles. One morning, I dramatically clung to a stop sign near the school. I hung on for dear life until my parents peeled me off the sign and carried me, kicking and screaming, the rest of the way.

Finally a decision was made to move me to the second grade. That did the trick! My second-grade teacher was a better match for me than my first-grade intimidator.

I've always had a heart for the underdog in any situation. I think my own experience as a helpless child with a threatening presence made me more sensitive to how it feels to be picked on or wrongly judged. And I certainly feel strongly about helping others in difficult situations.

Despite my rocky beginnings in Costa Rica, there were good times as well. My family became friends with the Dodds family—Crusade missionaries that remain some of our best friends to this day. When we weren't in school, Rachel and I played with their two daughters, Rachel and Michelle. Rachel was my age, while Michelle was my sister's age. It was a great match. The two Rachels were extroverts, while Michelle and I balanced out the foursome with our more introverted approach to life.

Our families would spend time traveling, sometimes taking excursions around Costa Rica together. I loved the ease of being with them and relaxing in the midst of adults and other children who spoke English.

Costa Rica is known for numerous rain forests and beautiful beaches. We visited both, but I loved the beaches the most. Huge turtles would come up onto some of the local beaches to lay their eggs, crawling across the sand until safely away from the tide. Then each turtle would use her back flippers to dig a big hole and deposit her eggs. When the eggs were hidden from predators and people, the mother turtles would crawl back to the ocean and swim off. After the baby turtles were born, they would also crawl across the beach and swim into their ocean home. We watched this entire amazing process together, thanking God for allowing us this glimpse into another part of his creation.

One of our excursions took us to an orphanage where we served as helpers. We four girls loved to play with the orphan children and love on them. It was obvious that their lives were nowhere near as comfortable as ours. The orphanage was situated in a big older home and held a bevy of children who were cared for by houseparents. Single beds and cribs were lined up against the walls in a plain dormitory-like room, nothing like the nice bedroom Rachel and I enjoyed.

The overwhelmed staff tried to give the children individual attention, but their time was so limited. We could tell that the children longed to be held, listened to, sung to, and just made to feel special.

I think I've always cared about other people. First I loved my dolls and then my real live baby sister. I loved Mom and Dad, the people close to me. I always wanted to help and nurture others, but now this innate desire expanded. When I met the children in the orphanage, their need for love and physical touch pulled me right in.

I got to know the poor children without parents and without any of the extras I enjoyed, and my heart ached for them. I wanted to hug all of them and fill them up with the kind of love that they might never have experienced but that I knew well in my home. The experience changed my heart.

After that, having compassion would become a bigger part of my life journey. I could thank Costa Rica for that. I didn't know until much later how much it all would influence my future path.

ANOTHER MOVE

After our eight-month assignment in Costa Rica, we moved back to Austin so my parents could work with college students from the University of Texas campus.

I'm so thankful that Mom and Dad weren't hypocrites who preached one thing and did another. They lived out their beliefs in front of us every day. They laid a foundation for our family built on faith in God and on the teachings found in the Bible.

But we weren't the only ones who benefited from their loving and gracious approach to life and faith. We regularly saw the impact our parents had on the lives of the students they worked with.

People were at our house at all times. Groups met for conversations about life issues, and sometimes their animated talks lasted well into the night as they discussed current events in the light of Scripture.

I loved to listen to and sometimes talk with these older kids about what they were learning. It was a stimulating time for this introverted little girl. They helped move me out of my shell a little bit.

I was going into sixth grade when Mom and Dad made another life-changing announcement: they'd taken a new assignment, and we were going to move to the quaint Mexican town of Xalapa in the state of Veracruz!

"No!" I complained. "I'll have to leave friends again and go to another school in a foreign country."

Then I learned that the school I'd attend was a Mexican school and Spanish was the only language spoken! How was I supposed to learn anything in a school where I didn't understand a word anyone said?

My parents calmly but firmly talked me out of my anxiety and assured me that I would learn the language the way many people learned foreign languages: by living in the midst of the culture and hearing it all day long.

My parents were right about me learning Spanish, and I quickly became fluent. My guardian angel during that time was a girl in my class named Cynthia. On the first day, she came up to me as soon as I walked into class.

I didn't understand all the words she said, but I couldn't miss the warm welcome she extended to me. Cynthia flashed a big smile, took my hand, and pulled me farther into the room. She waved to a few of the other girls who were her friends to come over and meet the new girl. They smiled and chattered their welcome to me.

Cynthia and her friends knew I couldn't understand their words, so they communicated with me with gestures and touch. I felt safe, despite the language barrier. Instead of me helping others, these gracious girls were helping me. They didn't ignore me and let me find my way on my own. I relaxed and smiled back, and by the end of the day, I looked forward to returning the next day.

Cynthia helped me through that first day and started teaching me how to say the pledge to the Mexican flag. When we went out to recess, a number of food carts lined the outdoor play area. Cynthia and I walked around and checked out the different offerings. Everything was freshly made and smelled wonderful. I pared my choices down to tostadas or empanadas, then finally settled on the empanadas.

The pastry turnover with pork filling reminded me of the good, authentic Mexican food back home in Texas. We ate under the shade of a nearby tree with some of Cynthia's girlfriends while some boys looked on from a distance. I felt like I fit in almost completely. My dark complexion and dark hair allowed me to blend in with the other girls. The main difference that made me an oddity was the language barrier, but that quickly changed.

I was fluent in two months, speaking almost as fast as the locals did and enjoying every minute. I loved learning about Mexican culture, especially how it inspired people to move their feet when spirited music filled the air. I enjoyed watching the children and adults dance in their colorful outfits when we attended birthday parties and special events. And I was delighted when I discovered that dance classes were part of our school curriculum.

The most memorable dance I learned was one requiring the dancer to balance a glass full of water on the top of her head. Gallons of cold water spilled over my shoulders while I was learning this maneuver, but I mastered it. By the end of the semester, I could dance gracefully and not spill one drop of the balanced water.

My confidence soared! Here I was, a girl who couldn't walk at first and then wobbled for a while, and now I was dancing with a glass of water on my head! Dancing felt so freeing that my introversion was overcome by the joy of moving to the rhythm of the music. I thanked God for the work he had done in my life and the joy I found in that Mexican school. I remember that dance to this day and can execute it beautifully, except with no glass of water on my head!

I had integrated so much into Mexican life—the language, the food, the joyful atmosphere of music and dancing—that I realized I had become part of Mexican culture, not just as a visitor who observed it from the outside but as someone who understood the people and their world.

I loved to be in the midst of the local people and feel a part of everything. Even going to a market with my mom was fun because I understood what she was saying to the vendors and what they said back to her. Sometimes they would speak directly to me, and I answered with confidence.

I often describe that time in Mexico as the happiest year of my childhood. I had grown and my confidence blossomed. And I learned something valuable: I wanted to know and love people who were different from me.

4.

AN EXPANDING HEART

. . .

WE MOVED BACK TO TEXAS AFTER I FINISHED SIXTH grade. Much as I loved Mexico, I was excited to get back to my friends and the same school I'd attended before we left Austin. Regents School of Austin is a private Christian school, and we were moving into our new house that was close by.

The first few weeks in Austin, I was getting used to living back in the States, but I realized I was dreaming in Spanish. It surprised me, and then I noticed that when I was talking during my waking hours, I often had to stop and mentally translate a word from Spanish to English. It took about a month for my mind to switch to thinking entirely in English.

School was a fun time of renewed friendships and lots of activities. I was the point guard on the A basketball team. Rachel, a year behind me in school, was the point guard on the B team. It was the only time I ever outdid her in sports. She continued to grow taller, and I did *not*. I'm five-foot-nothing!

We didn't have a formal graduation at the end of eighth grade, but the parents gave us a pool party and a little ceremony with certificates we could take home and frame. We didn't march to "Pomp and Circumstance," but we did line up, still in bathing suits, to receive our "diplomas."

Middle school had been wonderful, and the icing on the cake came in the form of a letter sent to our house at the end of the year. It was addressed to me. I held the envelope and wondered why my eighth-grade teacher, Nanci Boice, had written to me. She was my favorite teacher because she related to me with an understanding and connection that always made her class a joy.

I ripped open the envelope with great anticipation. As I read her words, tears welled up in my eyes: "If I had to return to the eighth grade, I would pick a friend like you to go with me."

The tears spilled down my face as I read line after line of compliments about my love for other students, even the ones who weren't always so loving and the ones who were often ignored for one reason or another.

Her closing paragraph became sealed in my mind and heart: "You were kind to the students that others considered unpopular, and you were not afraid to speak to them, even at the risk of your own popularity. I don't know if you noticed how appreciative the students were of your kind acts."

That letter touched me deeply. Ms. Boice got me. She understood who I was in the deeper part of myself. I wanted to be like her. I wanted to see who people were on the inside. Her insight confirmed the path that God would lead me to. I just didn't know yet how that path would unfold.

I moved up to James Bowie High School, where I was one of over two thousand students. I loved the hustle and bustle of its lively environment, and I got along with both the popular crowd and the kids who were more on the fringes. My world and my heart were expanding.

I was most involved with three Christian groups: my church

youth group, a Crusade high school ministry I started, and a Young Life group.

It seemed like I could move easily between the secular and Christian subcultures at school, so kids from differing backgrounds often came over to our house. Maybe I'd invite someone over after school to just hang out for a while or have several girls for a sleepover. My parents were always favorites with anyone who walked through our door. My mom would bake brownies and chat with whoever came. She'd ask them about school or what they liked to do in the summers. Both Mom and Dad were very welcoming to my friends.

A lot of the kids who came over would later comment on how their parents weren't like mine. They'd tell me that their parents didn't make brownies for them or ask them about their lives. They just loved the attention and care my parents showed to everyone.

My friends may have loved it, but it irritated me. I saw that the kids in homes where parents weren't so involved in their lives had something I wanted—freedom. It seemed their parents would let them make mistakes and learn from the mistakes. That sounded good to me.

I was taught what was right and what was wrong. There was no room to choose to make mistakes and learn from them. I knew that if I broke the rules, there would be consequences. But I decided to go ahead and see what the other side of life looked like. I was determined to find out what those kids had that I didn't have.

I decided to go to a party where I knew there would be drinking. My parents would definitely not approve. Then I told them I was going to spend the night at a friend's house, breaking the rule of "Thou shalt not lie." Two boundaries broken in one night! Well, I did actually spend the night at my friend's house. But *first* we went to a party, and then we went back to her house—well past my usual midnight curfew.

I wanted to be part of what was going on at the party. I didn't want to be seen as the goody-goody who never disobeyed her parents. I don't really know whether the parents of the kid who threw the party were home that night or not. He could well have been breaking rules that night too. I certainly didn't see any adults in or anywhere near that house.

Someone brought Smirnoff Ice as the drink of choice. Breaking the third rule of the night, I casually went over to the drink table, picked up a bottle, and took a swig. If I wasn't allowed to be at a party with drinking, I certainly wasn't allowed to actually drink alcohol. It tasted okay, but it wasn't a huge thrill. I must have got away with my deception because I don't remember any consequences.

I pushed some other boundaries in high school but chose not to expand my behavior into things more rebellious. While my parents could be considered strict, they were kind and openhearted.

At that point, I was just beginning to struggle with the tension that exists between the church and the world outside the church. I recognized in myself both a compassionate heart and strong biblical beliefs. When I thought about some churches that seemed to shame members who had made mistakes, I wished that all churches would be safe and redeeming places for people to experience forgiveness and grace.

I also saw how the world in general often treated people who were somehow different. I felt sorry for those people who seemed to live on the edges of life, without friends or the warmth of a community. If someone's mental, physical, or situational issues made him or her different, many people would steer clear. Not me. I wanted every person to feel seen and loved. That's still a big part of who I am.

Reaching out to others became part of my life.

Gregory was one such person. He was autistic and attended special education classes. Many of his fellow students either ignored him or treated him cruelly. My friend Charlotte and I walked down the same hallway to the cafeteria every day for lunch. Most days Gregory would be sitting on the floor with his back against the wall, his legs pulled up, his arms wrapped around them, and his head down. A blush crept up the back of his neck as he struggled to eat his lunch in that position. We understood his embarrassment when some passing students hurled insults at him.

One day during senior year, Charlotte and I stopped to talk to Gregory. The redness on his neck deepened, and he barely lifted his head to look at us. We spoke to him for several days on the way to lunch; then one day we sat on the floor and began to eat with him.

Over the next few weeks, we ate lunch with him and encouraged him to relax and talk with us. Eventually he raised his head, took his hands away from his face, and started to talk. I remember him sharing his love of art. Soon he started to wave at us as he passed us in the hallways.

Gregory became a friend, and he still keeps in touch with me, Charlotte, and my family, occasionally calling one of us just to say hello. He sends us beautiful cards he's created and always remembers birthdays and special occasions. From time to time, my dad will pick him up and take him to dinner. Sometimes I take Gregory to dinner, but I think he really enjoys guy time with my dad.

As we've continued our friendship with Gregory over the years, we've been rewarded with his love and appreciation. "You are the best friends in the whole world!" he tells us.

My friendship with Gregory started when I was in high school, and so did my relationship with a young child, about 4 years old, with special needs named Riley-Jane. This little girl became a significant part of my life and played a big role in shaping my future. Caring for her ignited my desire to go into nursing and started me in the direction I would follow after high school.

Riley-Jane's mother, Gayle, was my babysitter when I was little. Years later, Gayle gave birth to Riley-Jane. I was a senior when Gayle called me with the news that her precious baby girl had been born with multiple disabilities: her muscles didn't function normally; her bones were soft; she had a tracheotomy; she was on oxygen and had a feeding tube.

Gayle said that the doctors didn't think she could experience a good quality of life. However, despite all her challenges, Riley-Jane's life seemed full of joy. Her parents wanted to nurture that apparent joyfulness and enable her to live as well as she could. They decided to ask me to be her caregiver as much as my schedule would allow. I was eager to help. Riley-Jane could do nothing for herself. I fed her, bathed her, dressed her, and just tried to help her feel loved and accepted.

Right away I saw the joy that her mother had talked about. As I rocked Riley-Jane, she would grin up at me, communicating without needing to say one word. I wasn't sure whether she could really see me, but something inside Riley-Jane generated a spirit of happiness that was awe inspiring. Her vulnerability and trust fulfilled and blessed me more than I could have ever imagined. I saw beauty that radiated from her soul, surpassing the usual physical definition of beauty.

Riley-Jane passed away a few years ago. It wasn't surprising to see so many people who had been touched by her life—and the lives of her parents—gathered to celebrate her. We released balloons into the sky and rejoiced that she was now with her creator. Her quality of life here on earth defied what the doctors had said, and I am grateful for the opportunity to have been blessed by Riley-Jane.

WRITING MY OWN STORY

After graduating from Bowie, I immediately started pursuing nursing at Texas Tech University, six hours away in Lubbock. My parents helped transport my stuff and get me settled in my dorm room. After hugging and saying farewell, I watched through a window as they drove away. Tears rolled down my face as their car got smaller and smaller until I couldn't see it anymore.

I was in a new phase of life. I would be growing up on my own, away from my parents and Rachel. It felt scary yet exciting! But I knew it was time for me to write my own story.

Navigating my new environment included joining a sorority. I looked forward to the fun I would have meeting new people at the sorority activities that were scheduled through the school year.

I dove right into school and enjoyed as many activities as I could. Our sorority's formal dinner was the night before the end of the school year. I was dressed in a long black dress as I sat behind the wheel of my car. I was getting ready to pick up my date, a boy who was like a brother to me. I'd asked him to the dance, and I felt good knowing that the date would be a relaxed one since he was just a friend.

I was slowly backing out of my space in the student housing parking lot when I got whacked by another vehicle. The jolt didn't hurt my car too badly, but it did a number on my body. I was slammed into the steering wheel, and my torso was squeezed between it and the front seat. It was one of my sorority sisters who had hit me, and she got out of her car and came over. She asked whether I was okay and apologized profusely.

"I'm fine," I assured her. "No big deal."

I pulled myself together, picked up my date, and headed to the location where a chartered bus would take all the partygoers to the dance venue. I still thought I was fine, just a little shaken by the car incident.

But as I got off the bus at the dance, I fell flat on my face. I don't know whether my leg gave way or I stumbled stepping off the bus, but I know the result. I was lying facedown on the ground with my precisely applied makeup smeared with dirt and grime.

I tried to get up quickly and act composed, laughing at my clumsiness. My date asked me whether I wanted to go get checked out after enduring two jarring blows to my body. I did feel a little fuzzy headed and shaky but told him I wanted to go in and dance.

It took only about thirty minutes to realize that I was not doing well. My date took me to the emergency room, but after several tests, the doctors sent me home. Their report: No broken bones. No serious aftereffects.

At least, that's what they thought. But the pain lingered for months, leading other doctors to determine that the fender bender and the fall had triggered chronic pain—pain that largely had lain dormant since my birth.

Later I learned that wearing foot casts for clubfeet could've damaged other parts of my body. I found out that sometimes twins experience developmental problems.

I also found out that my pain was different. I learned that the damage a baby endures during a failed abortion can leave significant emotional and physical trauma that doesn't reveal itself until later in life. Some doctors believe that the fight-or-flight response that's hardwired into all of us went into overdrive in me as I survived the abortion that took my twin. The physical damage and my resulting fight-or-flight response are responsible for lingering pain that was finally awakened in my eighteen-year-old body by the car accident.

Doctors have told me that I will live with this pain the rest of my life. It manifests itself as a throbbing ache all over my body. My hips, feet, back, and neck carry the worst of it. Traveling causes exhaustion that makes me feel like I've run a marathon.

I'm not glad to be living with these issues.

Sometimes I indulge in a pity party and cry out to God to please take the pain away. I privately go to him and ask questions that have no answers at the moment. *Why, God? Why me? Why?*

I know in my head that he really does love me and holds my well-being close to his heart. I know in my head that he is working in my life for good. I know in my head that his promises are many. It's my heart that struggles with why life isn't pain-free if God is both powerful *and* loving. My doubts drop in for the pity party, and the tension of living with unanswered questions pulls me down.

After a pity party drains my energy, I lift my head and tell God what he already knows. The party is over, and I am back to accepting his grace and mercy for my lapse into anxiety. Pretty soon my emotions have changed from self-pity to joy. I can't really explain how that happens. It's part of the mystery of how God works in my life. I'm grateful to be alive even with chronic pain. I know it increases the desire in my heart to help others who are in pain.

ANOTHER CHANGE

After my freshman year, my desire to go into nursing increased, but my desire to go back to Texas Tech did not. I had wanted to go far away from home and experience life on a large secular campus. Texas Tech was certainly that! The college party scene was new to me. It made my few high school drinking parties seem like kids' stuff.

I missed friends and family back home. And the news that chronic pain would now be a regular part of my life made me want to be near my doctors. I moved back home and went to Austin Community College for a year. I took classes I needed to get back into a nursing program before transferring to Blinn College in College Station, Texas. I would still be close enough to go to my own doctors and go home to see my friends and family.

When I moved to College Station, I took courses to be certified as a medical aide, which would permit me to become a caregiver to people who needed more intensive care, like Riley-Jane.

One of my first patients was Bill, a quadriplegic paralyzed from the neck down. He couldn't feed himself, dress himself, or bathe himself, so he needed total care. The work was a physical struggle. I stood only five feet short and weighed 105 pounds, but it was my job to maneuver all six feet, four inches of Bill so we could complete all his basic tasks. I put everything I had learned into practice with the same joy I had when caring for Riley-Jane and befriending Gregory.

I learned from these beautiful people that they have love to offer if someone will take the time to see it. Riley-Jane could not speak. Gregory had difficulty relating to others in culturally accepted ways. Bill was physically bound by his paralysis. But each one was created by God, and each one deserved the love and care we all long for. In return, they gave me so much fulfillment that my desire to continue pursuing nursing just grew and grew.

I knew God had a plan for me, and I gladly followed his nudging to continue along the path of nursing or special-needs care-giving. The giving I did seemed small in the big picture of life, but I knew that God uses small things in big ways. Though I wanted to grow and mature and be the young woman God wanted me to be, I had no desire to seek a visible presence outside my own circle of life.

5.

MEETING TONYA

. . .

G ROWING UP, I HADN'T THOUGHT MUCH ABOUT ME OR my sister being adopted. It was normal for us. My closed adoption never caused me to even think about trying to find my birth mother. All I knew was that life was full and my family life was wonderful. Then things changed.

My sister, Rachel, had never met her birth mother, Olivia, but they had corresponded over the years. Shortly after Rachel graduated from high school, my parents were going on a business trip to the city where Olivia lived. They asked Rachel whether she wanted to go along and possibly meet Olivia for the first time. She decided to go and meet her birth mother.

The meeting went well. Rachel had so many questions that needed answers, and she came back feeling good about herself and her identity.

I was happy for Rachel, but I didn't experience any desire to meet my own birth mother. My life was busy with school and work. Embarking on a search for a woman I didn't know just hadn't crossed my mind. At least, not yet.

Then, about four months after Olivia and Rachel met, Olivia

let our family know she was coming to Austin on a business trip of her own. My parents and Rachel arranged to meet Olivia for dinner, and they asked whether I wanted to join them. I eagerly accepted the offer and looked forward to getting to know the woman who had given birth to my precious sister.

The first time I saw Olivia, I was struck by how much she was like Rachel. They are both tall and thin with similar builds and extroverted personalities, and they share almost identical body language. They even slipped off their shoes and compared their feet. Both of them wear the same size shoes and have long, slim toes. We all laughed with them at this similarity.

We were sitting at a round table, giving me a clear vantage point to watch both Olivia and Rachel as they talked to each other and to the rest of us. They were so much alike. Their voices highlighted their extroversion and enthusiasm. They were comfortable being the center of attention, and I was grateful to quietly watch this joyful scene.

My thoughts drifted to how empty life would have been without my wonderful little sister.

No playing "orphanage" together.

No fighting over clothes.

No exotic adventures in foreign countries.

No everyday moments with my spirited sister.

My heart swelled with love for Rachel and gratitude that Olivia had placed her baby girl in our family. Rachel completed us.

I was struck by how brave Olivia had been. She made a choice in placing Rachel for adoption that must have been bittersweet. Her choice gave Rachel a life she wouldn't have had otherwise. I wondered what Olivia had felt as she went through labor and delivery and then went home without her baby.

I leaned over to Olivia and thanked her. She smiled at me with tears in her eyes.

I have a woman like this in my own life, I thought as I smiled back at Olivia. It was the first time I personalized my birth mother as an individual who chose life for me at whatever the cost had been to her.

I knew almost nothing about my birth, my birth mother, or her pregnancy. An image of her was starting to take shape in my mind, but it remained cloudy, inexact. Did she look like an older version of me? Or was there little physical resemblance, like the difference between Rachel's dark hair and Olivia's light hair? Did some of my physical ailments at birth come from a condition she had? What illness might I experience in the future that she had already lived through?

Was she even still alive?

I'd always thought that adoptees looked for birth parents because they were missing something essential in themselves. I never felt that. My parents filled my life with such love and care that I simply didn't have a sense of loss.

But meeting Olivia that day broke open a desire in me to thank my birth mother for choosing life for me. I thought of her as a real person with a name and a life and feelings and maybe thoughts that her child might struggle with feelings of abandonment.

I wanted to find her and tell her how grateful I was for her and her choice. I'd always thought positively about my birth mother. I'm sure that's because of my parents' attitudes. When Rachel and I were growing up, our parents told us about the book *Dear Birth Mother: Thank You for Our Baby.* And they told us about the letters they wrote to my birth mother when I was born.

I knew they felt a deep love for both my and Rachel's birth

mothers and were grateful that they placed us for adoption, making it possible to create our family. My parents respected the women who were unable to raise their babies and chose adoption for them. And I wanted to respect my mom and dad before deciding to go ahead and open the door to searching for my birth mother.

I wasn't nervous to bring up the subject with them, but at the same time, I knew I would not begin a search if they were the least bit hesitant. Thankfully, there was no hesitancy at all. Mom and Dad understood my feelings after meeting Olivia and supported me completely. Since I was twenty years old, I was over the legal age of eighteen and able to pursue a search for my mother. My parents and I talked about my taking the lead on it with their ongoing support.

I didn't recognize it then, but I had been navigating the normal process of becoming more independent. All my life I had relied on my parents for counsel, and I still do. But more and more I gained the confidence I needed to step into uncomfortable situations when it would have been easier to let my parents handle them for me.

Going off to college had felt uncomfortable, but I had an idea of what that first adventure would be like. I could picture myself living in a dorm, making new friends, studying subjects I was interested in, and looking forward to Thanksgiving break and other holidays with my family.

This time, I was opening a door to the unknown.

I was certain, despite my mixed emotions, that God wanted me to do this. And I knew my parents would be right there with me all along the way. I felt like a fledgling bird jumping out of the nest in the middle of a foggy night. I knew I wanted and needed to jump, but would I be safe? Would I fly or fall? It was scary and exciting all at once. My parents' support, my desire, and the nudging of the Lord gave me the wings I needed.

THE SEARCH

My family and I agreed the first step was for me to call Deaconess to see whether they could help find my birth mother. I was home for Christmas break, and Mom, Dad, and Rachel were in the living room with me as I got ready to make the call. I held my phone, looking back and forth between the keypad and them. I felt a mix of emotions, as I was about to take the first step of an unpredictable journey. I was excited and nervous. I replayed the questions I'd been asking myself since the dinner with Rachel and Olivia.

What if Deaconess couldn't find my birth mother?

What if they found her but she wasn't willing to have contact with me?

What if? What if? What if?

At one point, I put the phone back in my lap and looked at the three faces smiling at me. I could feel their encouragement and understanding as I prepared to open a long-locked door.

My life could get more complicated. It undoubtedly would. Why disrupt my life and the lives of the people in this room who loved me so much? With my phone still in my lap and my heart pounding, I closed my eyes and prayed. Immediately my birth mother came to mind. The strong feeling I had when I sat next to Olivia burst through my hesitation. I knew I wanted to make this call.

I looked at my family one more time. This time, I was smiling as I picked up the phone. I tapped in the number and put the phone to my ear.

Relief flooded my mind and heart as soon as I was transferred to Debbie, the caseworker on my adoption. She was still at Deaconess. Not only did she remember me, but she also told me that she was looking at a framed picture on her desk at that very moment. The photo showed me as a baby in my foot casts.

Apparently, I was special to Debbie in some way. She didn't tell me why, but there was a reason she still had my picture on her desk twenty years later.

Debbie told me she didn't know where my birth mother was but would start looking for her right away. "I'll call you as soon as I know anything."

It was mid-December when I made the call to Debbie. I stayed busy helping the family with preparations for Christmas, but I never let my phone out of my reach. I repeatedly checked it to make sure I hadn't missed Debbie's call. I played scenarios in my mind about how my birth mother might respond if we could reach her. Sometimes I imagined her being thrilled. Other times I pictured her fearful or angry.

My family and I spent a few days during Christmas at my aunt Jill's house in Houston, so life got even busier. The house was full of family and the usual festivities of the holiday season. Finally, on Christmas Eve, my phone rang. Debbie's name popped up! I answered right away, my heart racing.

"I found your birth mother!" Debbie told me. She said she'd found her, called her, and asked a simple question: "Does the date March 6, 1988, mean anything to you?"

"Yes! Yes!" the woman said. "I've been waiting for this call for twenty years!"

Debbie told me that my birth mother agreed to talk to me and said that I could call her.

"Her name is Tonya," Debbie said at the end of our call.

"Tonya," I said softly as I hung up.

From that moment, Tonya became real to me, not a mysterious, unknown woman. The fourteen-year-old girl who gave birth to me was now a thirty-four-year-old woman. I wondered whether she had ever told anyone about me or whether she would tell anyone now. What had her life been like for the last twenty years? Now I had a phone number that might answer those and many other questions.

My family stood watching me and waiting for whatever news Debbie had given me. I smiled and told them that I would be making another phone call to a woman named Tonya! We hugged one another as I began to absorb the reality of this next step in my journey.

Even though I was emotionally exhausted, my mind kept switching on and off through that night. I kept repeating "Tonya." Questions about what she was doing filled my mind. Was she lying in bed somewhere thinking about me? How could she not be?

She was only fourteen when I was born! It must have been so difficult to find herself pregnant at such a young age. Tonya told Debbie that she had been waiting for that call all those years since my birth. I wondered whether she was now regretting that she said I could contact her.

After a restless night, I woke up to the realization that it was Christmas morning! What a present I had received the night before with Debbie's call, and what a lot of mixed emotions I now carried.

I love Christmas, and I love my family . . . but I had a hard time focusing on either of those things. I think everyone felt somewhat the same. It was the biggest family holiday of the year and the second biggest day in the Christian calendar. Jesus Christ was born, and I was dealing with the story of my own birth. I was grateful, excited, expectant, and exhausted.

I decided to wait to call Tonya until we got back home to Austin. She would be celebrating Christmas, too, and needed her own space to think about what was about to transpire.

HEARING TONYA'S VOICE

It was after the first of the year, and once again I held my phone, my feelings similar to those I'd had when I called Deaconess to ask about finding my birth mother. It had been less than a week since that call, and now I was going to actually speak to my birth mother. This time, however, I was much more nervous. Would Tonya tell me the whole story about her pregnancy and my birth as soon as she answered, or would she be silent? Would she be happy or sad, calm or angry?

I just couldn't settle the conflicting thoughts that were preventing me from making the call. *What's the worst thing that can happen?* I finally asked myself. My answer was simple. If the call went badly, we would hang up and never speak again. That would be disappointing, but I could handle that.

And if the call went well? Who knew what that might mean? Either way, I was ready for the next step in this exciting adventure. I remember the first few moments of that call word for word.

"Hello?" said a voice when someone picked up the phone.

"Hello. May I please speak to Tonya?"

"This is Tonya."

I could hardly believe the words I heard. They sounded like I had said them. Her voice was just like mine. For a brief moment, her name filled my mind. My birth mother was a real person. She was Tonya.

"Hi," I said. "My name is Claire."

"Hi, Claire," Tonya said in a subdued voice.

I chuckled to myself. She sounded pleasant but calm. Just like me! Even when I'm nervous, I appear laid back and unruffled. The excitement I feel shows up slowly, and that is exactly how the phone call happened.

I asked her about her current life. Was she married? Did she have kids?

She answered and asked me similar questions. When she told me that she was a nurse, I chuckled to myself again. I felt a second moment of identifying with her. Then her excitement broke through her calm.

"Claire, I was so thrilled when Debbie found me and called to see if I would be willing to have you contact me! I told her that I had been waiting for that call ever since you were born."

I let out a sigh of relief as Tonya went on. "I always secretly hoped you would look for me," she said. "But I was terrified I would let you down." Her voice trembled.

I wondered what would be terrifying to her, but I said nothing.

"I am so happy to finally talk to you," she said as her excitement seemed to return.

We exchanged a few more general comments, and then I asked her whether we could meet personally.

Tonya hesitated. I held my breath in the silence as time slowed down.

"Okay," she said.

We briefly discussed logistics and decided to check with our families on the scheduling. A few more phone calls settled the place and time. We would meet in Dallas in March 2009, the month I would turn twenty-one.

Tonya would be driving from Oklahoma, so we decided that my family and I would drive up to Dallas so she wouldn't have so far to go. Most of our logistical arrangements during those months were via text or email. They were perfunctory. Neither of us shared details about our lives over the past twenty-one years. I would be meeting Tonya without any of my questions about my birth or her pregnancy answered. I think I knew it would be better to hear them in person, and she must have felt the same way.

My emotions continued to fluctuate, but classes and work at the hospital kept me busy. I was the one who initiated the communications about our meeting, and I wondered whether Tonya would actually go through with it when March rolled around.

She kept responding to my texts and emails, so my family and I made plans to go to Dallas as scheduled.

Mom, Dad, Rachel, and I drove from Austin to Dallas to stay with Ethan and Janet Pope, friends of my parents. They had lived near us back when Mom and Dad adopted me. Mom says it was Janet who helped make my first bottle. They were excited to be part of this reunion and had agreed to let our family meet Tonya's family in their big living room.

Ethan and Janet were beaming when they greeted us at their front door. We hugged and chattered, and conversations spilled over one another until we finally settled down. I pictured them sharing the joy my parents felt when they took me home, and now they would be hosting the meeting of Tonya and me.

We all prayed together and thanked God for his marvelous presence in our lives and his ways that are beyond our knowing. As we sat around the dinner table, I told Ethan and Janet how the meeting the next day would happen.

Tonya would be driving to Dallas with her husband, Bryan, two of her three daughters, and her friend Romy. Romy was the friend who had walked with my mom through her pregnancy, my abortion, and my birth all those years ago. She was still standing beside Tonya, supporting her.

All evening I expected to hear from Tonya about her arrival in Dallas. She and the others with her would be staying in a hotel, and Tonya and I would decide on a time for everyone to come over to the Popes' house the next day. But my phone stayed silent. I kept checking, but no more texts from Tonya.

We all went to bed, but I couldn't sleep for fear I'd miss a text. I worried that Tonya had changed her mind and wasn't coming at all. In the darkness of night, I filled the hours of waiting with all kinds of questions. Should I have even asked her to meet me? Will we ever meet her if this meeting doesn't happen? Can I let go of this desire to meet her and thank her in person if I never have the chance to do that?

Finally, at 1:00 a.m., my phone lit up with a text message. But it was bad news for me. Tonya needed one more day to process her feelings about our meeting. She would get back to me about a time to meet the next day. Would it be okay to have our scheduled meeting one day later?

Of course I agreed. What else could I do? But that meant the waiting would go on for the rest of that night, the next day, and another long night.

Nagging doubts that had stayed mostly beneath the surface of my mind reared their heads during that long day and the next night. My family and the Popes loved on me and helped me hang on to hope that Tonya would not back out of our meeting. I was in the middle of the fog, but I was not alone. I knew I would be okay no matter what happened, but the hours did drag on and on.

A text from Tonya did come at last, and we decided to meet at eleven o'clock the next morning. I didn't feel like I had slept at all that night as I got up and went through the motions of usual morning activity—drinking coffee, getting dressed, nibbling at a piece of toast, joining the others after they had all done the same things.

The air in the Popes' living room seemed supercharged as we waited for the arrival of Tonya and her family. Nervous energy almost crackled through the air. We women chattered away about where to put this chair or that knickknack, while my dad and Ethan seemed to just be moving from one room to another.

We all laughed as we fussed over what kind of music to play in the background. I don't remember what we decided, and I'm sure no one noticed once the time came for Tonya to arrive.

I would be the one to answer the door. The others would be standing behind me. Beyond that, we had no idea what would happen. It all depended on how Tonya responded to facing the young woman she gave birth to twenty-one years ago.

As the mantel clock ticked toward 11:00 a.m., I stood in front of the closed front door. My family and Ethan and Janet stood behind me. We must have looked like actors placed in our positions for the first scene in a movie.

My heart raced; my hands twisted; my mind and heart filled with anticipation. In every part of my body, I carried the imprint of the woman who would stand on the other side of the door.

How would I process that reality? How would she?

The clock chimed eleven times. We waited, but not for long. The doorbell pierced the silence in the room, and a collective gasp startled us all into action. I stepped forward and put my hand on the doorknob. I turned it, opened the door, and saw Tonya for the first time.

No one moved. Her family behind her and my family and the Popes behind me watched as the weight of the moment surrounded us. I took a deep breath, smiled, and moved toward a woman who looked like I would in ten years. It was like looking in a mirror to the future. Tonya was my height and had dark brown hair, olive skin, and a smile that resembled mine.

Her four-year-old daughter, Payton, stood next to her, and even she resembled me at that age. Her husband, her teenage daughter Alex, and her friend Romy stood behind her.

Tonya returned my smile and moved into my arms. We hugged for what seemed like a long time. When we stepped back, the others around us relaxed enough to move into the room and be warmly greeted by the group inside.

Introductions were made all around, accompanied by handshakes, smiles, and some awkward laughter. My parents and Tonya cried, and I cried for them. I couldn't imagine the complicated emotions those three people felt as they met for the first time.

I watched them, feeling so much gratitude for my parents. They loved so well and showed grace so freely. Their attitude toward Tonya showed God's love as the three of them embraced.

I was completely open to whatever relationship might come about. But as I watched tears stream down their faces, my heart was full of love for these three parents who had found a way for God to work in our lives, first to create our family and now to bring us all together.

After the greetings and tearful hugs went so well, everyone decided we should go out for brunch. At the restaurant, our table had an energetic, nervous buzz as my parents passed around photos of me growing up and told one story after another.

Tonya and Bryan sighed fondly over each story. And as the adults were smiling and eagerly chattering, I visited with Tonya's two daughters, Alex and Payton, to make sure they didn't feel left out.

The conversations around the table continued. Tonya told us how she had picked my parents to be her baby's parents out of a big book full of photos the staff at Deaconess gave her. The photo album showed couples looking to adopt.

"I chose your family because I thought Warren looked kind and loving," she said. "I knew he would be the kind of father I never had."

She also told how Bryan, her wonderful husband, had rescued her out of a difficult situation. Tonya had been married with two daughters when that marriage fell apart. Bryan married Tonya and committed himself to loving and caring for her and her two girls.

Meanwhile, my dad and Bryan talked about guy things: their mutual interest in hog hunting and their undying love for the piney woods of Texas.

After the initial burst of energy I felt in meeting Tonya, numbness set in. I was so overwhelmed that I couldn't really focus on any one thing. It was easy to talk with Tonya's daughters, but I didn't even begin to comprehend that they were my half sisters.

With everything that was going on, I never noticed that my mom and my birth mom had an extended private conversation. Before long, I would find out how consequential that conversation was.

6.

A LIFE-CHANGING
REVELATION

. . .

Tonya and I continued to stay in touch. We decided it would be nice for me to visit her in her home in Yale, Oklahoma. It had been about two months since our first meeting, and I still had a lot of questions I wanted answers to.

As I sat on the plane, I stared at the blank inside page of the greeting card in my hand. The flight attendant had just announced, "We will be landing shortly. Fasten your seat belts, and stow your carry-on luggage under the seat in front of you."

What will I write? I silently asked myself.

I'd been holding that card for ten minutes! My mind was racing. The card was for Tonya, who would be picking me up at the airport in just a few minutes.

Suddenly the plane screeched onto the runway. The card in my hand bumped against the seat in front of me as I lunged forward, and I knew my time was up. I had to write something on that card . . . but what? I wanted to say so much. The words that Tonya would read needed to convey my deepest feelings in one or two lines.

I settled back in my seat and put pen to paper:

Thank you for choosing life for me.

Love, Claire

The card I'd labored over had been in my purse along with a necklace and ring with my aquamarine birthstone in them. I'd purchased these special gifts for Tonya. Everything I was about to do felt completely strange. I was traveling alone and staying in the home of someone I hardly knew. I would be meeting her entire family, who would have just found out about my existence.

If *normal* meant feeling like I'd felt before meeting Tonya, I would never have the carefree experience of living a normal, uncomplicated life again. I had suggested this visit and now wondered what, exactly, my new normal would be like. Had Tonya really wanted me to come see her in her own environment, or had I persuaded her to invite me? Would we be uncomfortable the whole time?

We'd been texting back and forth since our first meeting. Sometimes we had brief phone conversations, usually initiated by me in an attempt to get answers to my still-unresolved questions.

I'd begun to notice that Tonya would change the subject whenever I asked about my birth. She seemed uncomfortable and even a little anxious, talking in circles and unfinished sentences. I reminded myself that she had been only thirteen when she got pregnant. Maybe she was so traumatized that she didn't want to revisit that time in her life. I didn't want to push her over a painful emotional edge.

Finally I suggested we meet again, thinking that talking face to face might be easier for her than communicating remotely. She agreed and invited me to come stay with her and her family. We settled on a date around the end of May.

Ding. The sound indicating we could get out of our seats startled me. I put the card in the envelope, stuffed it in my purse, and joined the other passengers in the jam-packed aisle.

Even though I had written a kind sentiment on the card, I still agonized over how Tonya would receive it. I wanted her to know that God had pieced together all the parts of her story and my story to give me a wonderful life. I never felt any anger toward the birth mother I hadn't known. I'd been adopted by the most loving couple imaginable. Tonya's decision had resulted in me living a blessed life. My hope was that Tonya would feel the same love and grace in her life that I felt in mine.

The heat of Oklahoma City in May hit me in the face as the airplane door opened to release the passengers into the Jetway. I knew that Tonya would be waiting on the other side of security to pick me up and drive us back to her home.

I saw her immediately in the greeting area with Payton holding her hand. Payton ran up to me and hugged me while Tonya smiled and hugged me too. Payton took my hand with a little skip in her step as we walked out to the car. I looked down at this precious child and considered the resemblances to myself. Her hair color was blond to my dark brown, but her face still looked like mine at that age.

We did some window-shopping in the little town of Stillwater before heading to Yale, about fifteen miles away. Tonya pointed out a fabric store and excitedly talked about her love of quilting. Payton kept her hand tucked in mine as she danced along, singing and twirling as I spun her around. She seemed thrilled to have another big sister.

The town could have been a movie set for an old western. The one main road through town was just two lanes with small shops along each side. No crowded streets with honking cars or agitated drivers. Its charming quaintness was a stark contrast to Austin or Dallas and made for a pleasant break before driving on to Yale.

The road narrowed and turned from asphalt to gravel to a dirt driveway up to Tonya's front door. We pulled up to the house as Bryan and Alex came out to greet me. Bryan welcomed me warmly as we went inside. Alex smiled and gave me a hug, but there was no sign of Tonya's oldest daughter, Whitney.

I wondered how Whitney would receive me. Tonya had let me know that Whitney had been upset when Tonya told her about having had a child so many years before. She'd called her mother names and refused to come to Dallas on that first visit to meet me. Her mother's teenage situation must have shocked Whitney, but I had no idea how she'd feel about me. I felt bad for her and hoped to smooth any rough waters between us during my time in their home.

Bryan showed me to the bedroom where I'd stay for the next two nights. He was as warm and gracious as he had been when we met before, and I was grateful for the ease he seemed to feel with me. As I unpacked my bags, I noticed a beautiful quilt on the bed that I assumed Tonya had made.

We gathered back in the living room, and almost immediately Whitney appeared from the hallway. She had apparently been asleep, and she came out with half-opened eyes and hair spilling around her face. Tonya introduced us, and Whitney greeted me with a warm smile. She didn't say anything, but there was no apparent tension. I didn't need to worry about how she felt about me. I could tell that she had worked out her feelings enough to be pleasant.

I noticed that we all were pretty laid back, talking quietly, smiling—just a roomful of introverts hanging out. I definitely saw some personality resemblances between my birth mom, my half sisters, and me. We didn't need to fill the silent spaces with chatter like my extroverted sister, although at times I wished Rachel had been there because she would have broken the silence and won over the room with her contagious laughter and gift of storytelling. Still, I did feel a sense of contentment and familiarity.

At one point, Tonya proudly called me over to the corner of the living room where her sewing machine sat on a table with fabric and materials on a nearby shelf. She handed me a folded quilt. She was smiling and seemed happy.

"I made it for you," she said. "All the stitching is hand sewn."

She unfurled a beautiful yellow, black, and white quilt crafted in an intricately stitched floral pattern. I gathered it into my arms and pulled Tonya into a warm hug.

"It's gorgeous," I said, still holding her close.

The rest of the day continued to be an easy time as I helped the family get ready for a large gathering that evening with Bryan's family.

Bryan's parents, along with his brothers and their wives, came over that evening. They all greeted me with smiles and hugs and expressed how glad they were to meet me. The atmosphere was so friendly and tension-free that I felt more relaxed than I could ever have expected with such a large group of strangers. The gathering ended early, so Whitney and Alex went to see some friends. Tonya put Payton to bed, and Bryan turned in early too.

The whole evening, I'd been looking forward to giving Tonya the card I'd written along with the necklace and ring with my birthstone, an aquamarine, in each. Now with everyone cleared out, Tonya and I were the only two people left in the living room. She was sitting in a La-Z-Boy chair.

I walked to her chair, knelt beside her, and handed her the card and the box with the ring and necklace in it. She took them with a smile and put the card in her lap. The aquamarines sparkled as she opened the box and asked me to help her put the necklace on.

"It's beautiful, Claire," she said as she started to open the card. "The ring is beautiful too. Thank you so much."

I was excited and hoped the words I had written in her card would help her feel good about herself. She smiled at the image on the front of the card of a lovely front porch with flowers and rocking chairs on it.

But when she opened the card and read it, everything changed. Tonya's face contorted in anguished pain. Tears filled her eyes and came rushing down her face. She jumped up out of the chair, grabbed my hand, and led me toward the guest bedroom.

As soon as we were in the room, she closed the door and pulled me down to sit next to her on the bed. I looked at her face and saw such deep distress. Her expression seemed to scream for help as she lowered her head. She was already crying and was soon sobbing and shaking. She was trying to calm down enough to say something. Whatever it was, I knew I was about to hear an unspeakably traumatic part of Tonya's story related to my birth.

I couldn't imagine why she was shaking and crying in such fear. I obviously knew she had gotten pregnant and placed me for adoption. What else could she have to reveal that would be so bad? I felt my own anxiety and confusion growing. What had happened?

From the time Tonya picked me up at the airport until the moment she opened my card, everything seemed fine. Now she was completely undone and struggling to bring her emotions under control.

I put my arm around her and held her. Finally her shoulders relaxed and her gasping settled into heavy breathing. Then Tonya lifted her head and turned to me, ready to tell me her story. Our story.

With tears in her eyes, she began. "I was thirteen when I got pregnant and had just turned fourteen when you were born. What happened isn't what you think happened." She paused. "I didn't choose to give you life."

I slid my arm off her shoulder as my breath caught in my throat. I could hardly believe what I was hearing. *What?* I thought she'd chosen to give me up for adoption. I was so confused.

"When I told my mother I was pregnant, she was furious," Tonya continued. "She was ashamed of me and immediately told me that I would have to have an abortion and tell no one about getting pregnant. The only person I told was my friend Romy, who came with me to meet you that first time. I didn't even think about what I could do differently. I was barely a teenager, and I saw no option but to obey my mother. The day she took me to a clinic that performed abortions, I was terrified. I was about twenty weeks pregnant, and all my mother could think about was 'getting rid of the problem.' She thought of you as a problem and my behavior as so shameful that it needed to be fixed and hidden forever."

My heart was pounding. So many thoughts spun in my brain at this shocking news. Tonya reached for my hand. I squeezed her hand and nodded for her to go on.

"My mom stayed in the waiting room while I was taken into the room where I'd undergo a procedure to remove my baby from my body and my life. I was alone and scared. The doctor never said a word to me. It was as if this were just another day in the life of a bad young girl. An assistant held my hand and said things I can't remember. The doctor did whatever they do to take a baby out of a mother's body. Getting up and back into my mother's car is a blur. I just remember being so upset that I couldn't think straight.

We went back home, and my mother informed me that I would go to school the next day and this whole episode would never have happened. No one else knew. No one else need ever know. I did what she told me. But pretty soon I realized that my stomach was still growing. I missed another period and began to wonder if they hadn't really gotten my baby out of my body after all. I had to tell my mother, as much as I dreaded the explosion that I knew would follow."

I put my arm back around Tonya's shoulders and held her tight. I saw this grown woman tucked under my arm as a thirteen-year-old girl, scared, with nowhere to turn but to her angry, cruel mother.

Tonya drew in a shaky breath. "Though a few more weeks had gone by, my mother hurried me right back to the doctor and demanded to know what was going on. After examining me, the doctor said that I had been carrying twins. They aborted one twin but didn't know the other one was there. My mother was so irate. She screamed and yelled and told the doctor, 'We can't let the little whore get away with this! It will embarrass the whole family! Get rid of it.' The doctor told her that it was illegal in Oklahoma to perform an abortion in the third trimester, so he could not go ahead with the procedure. He knew that it was still legal in Kansas, however, so I was hustled across the state line to have another abortion. Another doctor, another frightening, cold, sterile table, another terrible humiliation, and my mother who was even angrier than she had been the first time I faced this horror."

Tonya stopped talking and just sobbed. I could see that every tear, every knot in her throat as she gasped for another breath was the result of the trauma she had carried in her body all those years. Every muscle tensed as she relived that time in her life.

For the first time I realized that a woman experiencing an abortion was a real person. And Tonya did give me an amazing life by placing me for adoption. She'd had a rough upbringing in a divorced home, but she'd given me what she wanted herself . . . a loving, supporting, and accepting family. I could look at her with gratitude instead of judgment.

Finally Tonya's breathing calmed, and through tears, she smiled at me. "But your life was spared one more time. When your twin was aborted, the sac had been ripped. It was too dangerous to abort you. You lived!"

Then, with tears flowing again, she said, "Claire, I am so deeply sorry for aborting your twin."

I hugged her and told her I forgave her.

Before we came into this room, I had seen Tonya as a woman who had had a difficult time as a very young teen but was now happily married with a family of her own. Now I saw that inside she was really broken and hurting. I felt sorry for her but also knew I had just received a revelation that changed the story of my own life in ways I could have never imagined.

Tonya hugged me and thanked me and left the bedroom. She was as exhausted as I was confused. There was so much to absorb and process. I stayed sitting on the bed for a long time. Finally, like I'd done in the past, I asked God to be with me.

With his assurance, I was able to get up and do the next best thing to make it through the shock I'd received. I called my parents. My parents were not surprised when I told them what had happened.

"We already knew," Mom told me.

She went on to explain what Tonya had told her when she visited Dallas. While we were all at the restaurant, Tonya quietly told my mom about the abortion of my twin and the attempted abortion of me. My parents thought it was better not to say anything right away and see whether Tonya would tell me on this visit.

I was relieved that they hadn't told me earlier. They had had six weeks to think about this new part of my story. Now that I knew, they wanted to see how I was dealing with it.

"I don't know," I told them. "It doesn't seem real. I just can't wrap my head around it."

PART TWO

...

Writing a New Story

7.

THE UNRAVELING

. . .

SHOCKED.

Confused.

Lost.

Upended.

That's how I was feeling after learning that much of the story of my life that I had grown up with wasn't true.

When I traveled alone for my second meeting with Tonya, my goal was to thank her for choosing life for me and placing me for adoption. But Tonya let me know that wasn't the way things had happened.

The truth was Tonya *hadn't* chosen life for me. The words I wrote in that card earlier in the day had unlocked a world of emotions in both of us. I now had to face the startling reality that I was almost aborted . . . twice.

I didn't know where to even begin unpacking my new, more complicated life story.

I felt like I was riding a roller coaster that was speeding up and down as it took me through two separate territories: my old story of who I was and the new information that had made my old story so incomplete.

I can tell you that even today, years after the sudden revelation, it's still hard to fathom it all. There are moments when I look back into my old, familiar life story and question the new version of me. *Maybe all this didn't really happen*, I sometimes think. I know that it *did* happen, but the overwhelming tension between the reality I had lived and the true reality is sometimes too much to unravel.

When this happens, I usually call my parents. I am a very family-oriented person. I talk to my parents every day. Some people think my behavior is unusual for an adult, and some have even called me codependent. I'm not, but my parents are a kind of anchor in my life, constantly helping me understand what's going on and how to respond to challenges in ways that are consistent with who I am and what I believe.

When I asked them that night on the phone what they thought about Tonya's revelation, they told me how they had discussed it and prayed that I would be strong when I heard the news. They reminded me, as they had often done over the years, that help for any situation can be found in God's truth.

Sure, I needed to do some serious revisions to my life story. But as I reflected on my journey so far, it was clear that my life had much that was good and that these changes wouldn't tarnish this goodness one bit. I knew God still loved me, just as I am, with a deep and unfathomable love. I knew my parents still loved me, and in case I had forgotten, they reminded me once again.

"Always remember," Dad told me, "we wanted you, Claire. We chose you. And even though you're older now, we still love you more than anyone has ever loved a child."

Dad then suggested a different perspective on my unusual origin story.

"Look at it this way," he said. "God must have had a pretty big plan for your life to bring you through all of that to have you born. You're really supposed to be here!"

I was so grateful for my parents because I knew that not all adoptees experience the kind of life I had. They might not struggle with surviving an abortion, but they often face many challenges: a sense of abandonment, difficult relationships with their adoptive parents, difficult relationships with siblings, uncertainty about their origins. I was so comforted knowing I could turn to my parents as I faced this rather unusual challenge of my own.

AN AWKWARD LUNCH

Tonya had been worried that telling me the truth would ruin our new relationship. She feared I would be angry at her or hate her for getting the abortion that should have ended my life before it really began.

We were in the kitchen the next morning when she tentatively said, "Claire, I hope you still want to have a relationship with me."

"Of course I do," I said. She seemed relieved as we each went back to our rooms to get dressed for the final day of my visit.

I didn't feel the slightest bit of hatred for her. She seemed like a victim in the whole situation—abandoned by the boyfriend who had fathered me and pressured by her mother to quickly deal with the pregnancy. Her mother certainly had not given Tonya any options besides abortion.

I actually saw Tonya as exceedingly courageous. She bravely revealed to me her deepest, darkest secrets, things she had revealed to very few others over the years. She had little to gain from her naked honesty with me, but she had much to lose.

I was grateful for her trust in me. But the information she gave me made me feel like I was living in a dream or going through an out-of-body experience. It seemed I was outside my own life, looking in.

Tonya had told me the day before that we would be having lunch with her mother, Tonya's sister and her husband, and their two children. Also joining us would be her sister's son Stephen, who had also been placed for adoption at birth and was now in his early twenties. He and Tonya's sister had been reunited a couple of years before this lunch. He lived nearby, and they had grown their relationship over those two years.

My anxiety about this family lunch gathering was confirmed when Tonya gave me a brief warning. "My mother did not want you to be born," she reminded me, "so don't expect her to be too friendly."

I didn't and she wasn't.

Understandably, my appetite was smaller than normal as all of us sat down to lunch at Eskimo Joe's, a famous restaurant in Stillwater, Oklahoma. I never ate much of my hamburger.

I was sitting next to Tonya on one side with Payton on the other. Farther down were Tonya's sister and her sister's husband.

At the opposite end of the table was Tonya's mother, glaring at me. She acted colder to me than anyone else in the family did, but her aloofness was made up for by the warmest person at the table, Tonya's husband, Bryan.

I felt accepted by Bryan from the first time I met him. He smiles a lot, doesn't draw attention to himself, and communicates kindness with a nod of his head. At that first visit in Dallas, Bryan shed a tear more than once.

As we sat down at the table, he softly said, "How are you doing?" I nodded with a weak smile, letting him know I was okay. He smiled back in an understanding way.

I don't remember saying much as Tonya's family members talked. It seemed everyone was intent on avoiding any mention of my origin story. I wasn't sure whether Tonya had told her family all the details she had revealed to me.

Tonya's sister and Stephen sat next to each other and chatted easily. He was in the same relational position as I was as a fellow adoptee. He and Tonya's sister seemed to relate really well. They laughed together as I watched and wondered. Would that kind of relationship be in the future for Tonya and me? Would we be able to share laughter and life experiences as we spent more time together?

I could feel my love for Tonya growing. I was now twenty-one, and I could picture her two decades younger as a pregnant, fearful thirteen-year-old girl trying to do the best she could. I found myself wondering how I might have responded if I had been in Tonya's shoes. Would I have gone for an abortion like she had been forced to do?

I must confess, until that day, I never really gave abortion much thought. At that stage of my life, I had more pressing issues on my mind: transitioning to adulthood and starting my nursing career. And surprisingly, even though I was studying to pursue a career in nursing, I didn't know Planned Parenthood was an abortion clinic.

My parents recently reminded me that they had taken me along with them one day when they joined some fellow Christians to pray outside a Planned Parenthood clinic in Dallas. I was just an infant, so I don't remember that day. And I don't remember much talk about abortion in our household as I was growing up. We talked all the time about God, our faith, and Mom and Dad's work in evangelism and discipleship. But abortion? Somehow it wasn't really on our radar.

I did hear from some other kids that the churches they attended openly shamed girls who got pregnant. One friend even told me that she was in church one Sunday when a pregnant teenager was called up in front of the church and made to confess her sin. The girl admitted she had considered abortion because she was afraid of the very shame she faced in front of the church.

"Is this what Jesus would do?" I demanded to know. "This is not the way we want to respond to people facing the crisis of un-planned pregnancy. This is not how we should treat people. This is not the message we want to send about the love and mercy of Christ."

The friend who witnessed this scene was as upset as I was, but we both knew we couldn't do anything about it. One good thing to come out of this story is that I now have a powerful passion to challenge churches to be safe havens for men and women strug-gling with unplanned pregnancies.

I wanted church to be a safe place for any woman or man facing an unplanned pregnancy, but it wasn't safe, healing, forgiving, or redemptive. Today you can still find churches that are pro-life but aren't pro the people in their congregations who slip up. This is something I speak about whenever I get the chance.

I must also confess that there's one other thing I didn't know before Tonya told me the truth of my birth: I never knew someone could survive an abortion. I had always assumed the procedure was straightforward and effective. But now I knew things could be more complicated. And while I was grateful that I had survived, I felt all alone in a strange kind of way, alone in being the only per-son to survive an abortion.

I later learned I wasn't as alone as I thought. There are more than 270 documented cases of people who have survived abor-tions, according to the pro-life organization Susan B. Anthony List, which features me among the survivor stories on their site.[1]

For years, I believed that I was the only survivor of an attempted abortion of twins, or at least the only twin abortion survivor who was out speaking publicly about her experience. But I have since learned about other twin abortion survivors.

I had given virtually no thought to abortion before learning I was one of the fortunate few to escape its deathly grip. Now that I was able to see for myself the repercussions of the abortion that involved me, all I could see was the pain abortion causes.

On top of that, I realized that I had lost the brother or sister who grew alongside me during the five months we spent together inside Tonya's womb. I have the feeling that my lost sibling was a brother, but I won't know the truth about that until I get to heaven. I do know that I could picture the two of us lying next to each other, bumping up against each other, and even communicating nonverbally as we developed. If my sibling was a boy, and if my parents had adopted both of us, his name would have been Warren Culwell III.

When I was growing up, I always felt like someone who was missing a brother. I had a sister, and I loved Rachel with all my heart. But somehow, having a wonderful sister didn't remove the hunger I felt for a brother to love and grow up with.

Whether my twin was a brother or a sister, I'm looking forward to meeting my twin in heaven, where I suspect he or she has already made the acquaintance of Warren Dale Culwell Sr., my favorite person in the entire world, the man I lovingly called Granddaddy. And, of course, my beloved Gramps!

All my confusion about my past came at a time when I should have been preparing for my future. I was within sight of finishing at Blinn College and applying to nursing school. But now that my origin story was undergoing radical revision, processing all this new information consumed my focus and energy.

I asked myself, *If I'm not who I thought I was, am I still supposed to follow the career path the old me chose?*

I was confused and conflicted, and I worked through my confusion by spending time alone in prayer and time talking with other people. When I talked with God or my trusted friends, I asked questions: "What does this new reality mean for me? And what am I supposed to do with this?" I had additional questions specifically for God: *"What's your plan for me now? Is there something in my new life story that you can use for your purposes?"*

8.

MY YEAR OF DESTINY

. . .

*I*DRAGGED MYSELF BACK INTO MY APARTMENT IN COLLEGE
Station, Texas, after my visit with Tonya, and I plopped down on
the couch in exhaustion. I'd been gone only two days, but it felt
like so much longer. My thoughts were fragmented as I tried to
make sense of all I now knew about my own life. I looked out the
big picture window in my living room and remembered how happy
I'd been to see this feature in my little apartment when I moved in.
It gave me a perfect view of the gatherings that happened nearly
every day in front of the business located directly across the street.

My mind was drawn back to several months before when some
other significant events had taken place in my life. I had stood at
the window, watching, as cars entered and exited the parking lot. A
small group of people—some days just a few, some days a dozen
or so—would stand on the sidewalk. Sometimes the group would
say things to the people who came and went, and sometimes they
wouldn't. Every once in a while, one of them would hand a piece
of paper to one of the people visiting the business.

I didn't know who the people were or what the business did,
and I didn't really care. I only knew that I needed to be cautious

while driving to and from classes so I didn't hit any of the people lining the sidewalk. I didn't know it at the time, but I had moved into a neighborhood that was about to become ground zero in America's pro-life movement. A movement I knew little about.

I hadn't yet met Tonya, so I hadn't learned the story of my surviving an abortion. But once I learned my origin story, I saw my new neighbors in a different light. My apartment's address—the 4100 block of East Twenty-Ninth Street—put me right in the center of pro-life action. One Planned Parenthood executive called this area "the most anti-choice place in the country" for its opposition to abortion.[1] I didn't realize it then, but the business across the street was a Planned Parenthood clinic—and not just any Planned Parenthood clinic. By the end of the year, this clinic would become the most famous Planned Parenthood clinic in America. My geography was about to become my destiny!

Abby Johnson was the clinic director. She didn't know it yet, but her life was about to change just as radically as my own would. In rapid succession, Abby would quit her job, emerge as a powerful public face of the pro-life movement, and become one of my best friends.

I would also learn about those people I could see on the sidewalk every day from my apartment's picture window. They were sweet, loving people, mostly devout Catholics, who were connected to two small pro-life organizations I had never heard of: the Coalition for Life, a local group founded in the late 1990s, and 40 Days for Life, a national group that was founded in College Station in 2004 to organize a forty-day vigil of prayer, fasting, and outreach in front of the Planned Parenthood clinic.

These small, little-known local organizations were undergoing their own radical changes. Soon they would no longer be small, little known, or local. Instead, they would rapidly grow into major national and international organizations. Today, 40 Days for Life has more than a million volunteers around the world, and Pope Francis is among the group's supporters.

Our little neighborhood was about to enter a chaotic and eventful season that would forever change all of us. Our local group supported the national groups, and we were about to become almost as well known as they were. I didn't know then how that would happen, but I sensed that these committed people would have an impact in the pro-life movement.

Was I prepared for all that was about to happen? Probably not. But God knew exactly what was happening, and he led me every step of the way.

Four weeks after moving into my College Station student apartment, I ventured out one day to find out what the people I could see through my window were doing. My curiosity took over my timidity as I left my building. I wasn't afraid at all. The people who were outside the unknown business had never seemed to cause any trouble.

"Hi, I'm Claire from across the street," I said. "Who are all of you folks?"

Three or four kind elderly men and women greeted me. One of the men got up off his knees on the sidewalk to say hello and shake my hand. One of the women wore a crucifix on a chain around her neck.

"We pray for the women," the man said.

"We're pro-life," one of the women said. "We believe abortion takes the life of innocent children, and we want women to know there's another option."

She told me they were Catholics who were affiliated with the Coalition for Life, which had an office right next door to the Planned Parenthood clinic. I'd heard about Planned Parenthood, but it wasn't a group that I'd thought much about. Just like I hadn't thought much about abortion, I hadn't become familiar with the political issues surrounding Planned Parenthood.

"Are you pro-life?" another one of the women asked me.

"I guess I am," I answered. But her question surprised me. Nobody had ever asked me that, and frankly, I wasn't really sure what I thought. Of course, I was familiar with the term, but again, I just had so little exposure to the two opposing political movements.

At the time, I was definitely pro-adoption, but I wasn't sure I would call myself pro-life. If you had asked me then about my opinion of the pro-life movement or pro-life activists, I wouldn't have had much to say, other than noting that some of the pro-life activists I had seen on the news seemed angry. For me, their anger had drowned out their message.

But these people I was talking to weren't angry like the activists I had heard about. These people didn't shout at women who came to the clinic. They prayed silently and occasionally tried to speak to the women. My feelings about meeting them were mixed. I liked their kindness and sincerity, but I wasn't really sure what to make of them and their pro-life work.

STEPPING OUT OF
MY COMFORT ZONE

I was still thinking about that initial interaction as I went to the kitchen to get a cup of coffee. I had dozed off on the couch, and I needed something to clear my head so I could sort out my thoughts about my visit with Tonya. I turned on the Keurig coffee maker and waited for the blue cup buttons to start blinking.

With coffee in hand, I went back to the window and looked out. As usual, there was a small group in front of the clinic. Nothing had changed. But I was wrong. Something in me was beginning to wake up to what the people inside and outside that building were all about. Nothing was sorted out in my mind yet, but I was about to step into more personal discomfort than I could have imagined. Just not right away.

For the next several months, I focused on my studies as my mind and heart struggled to make sense of all I had learned about my origin story. I also kept my eye on the group of pro-life people across the street, and sure enough, over time my opinion of them shifted.

Initially I didn't know what to make of their work, but now I was sympathetic. I began to take the issue of abortion more seriously, and I was increasingly anti-abortion. Even though I had no interest in becoming a pro-life activist myself, I wanted to help these people praying in front of the clinic. So I hatched a plan.

I decided I was ready to go public with my story. I was shy and introverted, so I decided I'd let a sheet of 8½" x 11" paper do the talking for me.

I would make a simple flyer that told a bit of my story and featured photos of me with Tonya and my mom and dad. Then I would give copies of the flyer to the group in case they wanted to share my story with women seeking abortions. I had seen some of the other literature the group used, and I thought my story might offer more of a personal note that could connect with women who felt like abortion was their only option.

I worked on my flyer for weeks, getting some help from Mom, who had a library of family photos and was a real pro at putting together newsletters. I used the headline "Abortion, Adoption and Me," told bits and pieces of my story, and included ten color photos of me with Tonya, Mom and Dad, and Rachel.

"In March of 2009, when I was 21 years old, I met the most

beautiful woman I've ever seen, my birth mother," I wrote in my flyer. "She gave me the best gift I've ever been given, and that's the gift of life. I will always love her for that."

I wrote a bit about my wonderful experience as an adoptee and my shock at finding out that I had survived an abortion. "One was aborted, and one survived," I wrote. "I am a twin abortion survivor. It's a miracle!"

I closed with a plea to readers: "Although I don't know why I survived the abortion and my twin didn't, and I don't know why I was given the amazing, loving family that I was adopted into, I know this amazing story of life and being wanted by loving families should not be a rare thing! Other children can have the same gift of life that I have.

"Abortion is not the only option and I'm alive today because of this."

The flyer provided some information about how women could choose adoption over abortion and included contact information for the Coalition for Life and local pregnancy centers, as well as my own email address in case people had questions for me.

I took my flyer to Kinko's and asked them to print fifty copies in color. I wondered what the woman behind the Kinko's counter was thinking as she read the flyer and looked up at me. I smiled but silently prayed she wouldn't ask me anything. I really did want to help the women walking into the clinic, but this step felt so very uncomfortable. Was God really calling me to do this, or was I supposed to remain the observer behind the scenes instead of putting myself in the public eye?

The clerk at Kinko's didn't ask me anything. She just smiled and I smiled back. A few minutes later, I left with fifty flyers and headed for the people peacefully praying in front of the Planned Parenthood clinic.

I approached them to give them my flyers.

"Hi," I said. "I'm Claire from across the street. I met some of you in February."

One of the women remembered me and said hello.

"A lot has happened since February," I said, then briefly told them about how I learned I had survived an abortion that killed my twin.

"I thought these flyers about my story could help you reach some of the women going to the clinic. You can feel free to use these if you think they will help. I was hoping they might cause women to place their babies for adoption instead of having abortions."

My plan was to hand them the flyers and quickly return to my apartment and my studies. But when they heard my story, some of them had tears streaming down their faces. They were so enthusiastic that they invited me to come inside the Coalition for Life office and share it with some of the staff there.

Surprisingly, I gladly agreed. I didn't even hesitate. It felt good to be helpful. Once I was inside, I met Abby Johnson, who had resigned from Planned Parenthood the week before and was now working with the Coalition for Life.

One of the Coalition for Life workers thanked me for the flyers and invited me to join them as they prayed on the sidewalk and talked to the women.

"I might like to join you someday," I told her, but I also let her know I wouldn't feel comfortable talking to the women. My feelings about the whole subject were still too sensitive for me to try something like that.

It was interesting how my ideas were changing about what it meant to be pro-life. In February, when one of the people praying asked me whether I was pro-life, I wasn't sure. If they had asked me now what I thought, I would have answered without hesitation, "Of course I'm pro-life!"

I said goodbye and assumed that was that. I had told my story in the flyers I delivered, but I didn't plan on getting involved in pro-life activism. I had been studying the pro-life movement, and I didn't like everything I saw.

Some of what I had been seeing and reading was terribly upsetting. There was an angry pro-life contingent that, unfortunately, created a bad name for the whole movement and defeated the purpose of trying to save the lives of the unborn. I noticed pro-life people tended to fall into three groups:

- *Peaceful pro-lifers* like my friends across the street. These pro-lifers were kind. They showed love and respect to *all* lives, including the unborn, women facing difficult life issues, and even their critics.
- *Apathetic pro-lifers* like me. They said they were pro-life, but they didn't know, say, or do much about pro-life issues.
- *Angry pro-lifers* who noisily protested outside abortion clinics with graphic signs and bullhorns they used to shout hurtful words to the women entering the clinics.

As far as I could tell, the apathetic people made up the vast majority of the population. The peaceful pro-lifers were a much smaller group. But it was the even smaller number of angry ones who generated the most attention and condemnation.

I didn't intend to be an activist, but the more I read, the more I wondered what God had for me in all this. I got really interested in what these angry pro-lifers were doing besides yelling and tormenting others. I learned that some members of the pro-life movement will argue for killing abortion providers if that will save the lives of the unborn.[2] That's what Scott Roeder believed. In 2009, he killed George Tiller, who had become a target of pro-life activists because he performed late-term abortions. Roeder shot Tiller on a Sunday morning while Tiller was serving as an usher at his Reformation Lutheran church in Wichita.[3]

In 2015, another activist attacked a Planned Parenthood clinic in Colorado Springs. As a self-described "warrior for the babies," he injured nine people and killed three—one of whom was police officer Garrett Swasey. The officer worked for a nearby university and responded to the shooting. He was a copastor of a church called Hope Chapel and a former championship skater who left behind a wife and two children.[4]

In Alabama in 2019, one pro-life activist didn't use a gun. He used his car to try to run over an abortion clinic escort, one of several escorts needed to protect women from hostile activists.[5]

It was upsetting to hear and read about tragic protests. I didn't think they saved lives, and they hurt the pro-life message of preventing abortions while caring for pregnant women.

Fast-forward a few years, and I would have my own encounter with angry pro-lifers in January 2020 when I spoke at the Tulsa March for Life. Waiting for me in the crowd were two men yelling into bullhorns. One was screaming verses from the New Testament, while the other yelled that the pro-life movement had blood on its hands because it hadn't yet succeeded in abolishing abortion through legislation.

The two men directed their comments at me when I gave my message about God's love and forgiveness for women who've had abortions. As I was talking about grace and redemption, they were talking about condemnation and hellfire.

I spoke to the two men after my message was over. "I don't appreciate what you're doing, because there are so many women here who are hurting, who regret their abortions, who have found redemption and healing in Christ because Christ has wiped their slates clean."

"So, have you ever seen one of those murder mills?" one of the men asked me.

"Yes, I have," I said. "You may say you're preaching the gospel, but I don't hear Jesus's call to save the lost. All I hear is you condemning every single person here when we should all be on the same team fighting abortion."

I was trying to be truthful and direct, but I didn't want to shame them and bully them the way they were doing to me. Giving it back to them just like they give it out isn't the best way to handle difficult people.

"Would you please stop and please leave?" I asked them.

They were untouched and continued ranting and raving about murderers and blood and holocaust.

The pro-life movement has its share of activists engaged in behavior that fails the basic "what would Jesus do?" test. Yes, they make a lot of noise and grab a few headlines, but their approach isn't helpful because their hate for those involved in abortions leaves no room for the love of God.

One powerful reason I worry so much about angry pro-lifers is Tonya. I think about the torment she endured after becoming pregnant at thirteen. I never would have wanted Tonya to encounter angry pro-life activists calling her a murderer, saying she had blood on her hands, or telling her God condemned her for her choice.

I do wish Tonya had encountered people like the peaceful pro-lifers I met. They were loving, compassionate, and respectful. They prayed more than they talked. And when they did talk, they didn't shame or condemn women. They said, "We love you, we know you are scared, but you do have another choice, and we can help you."

While a handful of angry pro-lifers do terrible things, they do not represent the people I came to know. My interest in the pro-life movement grew as I interacted with these loving people and began to understand their goals.

It didn't take me long to realize I wanted to pray with my friends on the sidewalk. Before I could do that, though, I needed to go through the training that the Coalition for Life required of all its sidewalk counselors. I learned how to behave, what to say, what *not* to say, and how to offer my flyer to anyone who might be interested in my story.

Without the training, I might have chickened out at some point. It can be scary to approach women who may not want to talk to you. I so wanted to show my love for them and not shame them. I learned how to be polite and kind and to sincerely pray for these women making such a crucial decision.

Some days I prayed alongside my three friends from the coalition: Abby Johnson, Heather, and Karen. We grew closer as we spent time on the sidewalk, at meetings, at outreach events, or enjoying lunch together. Heather and Karen were combined into one character in the movie *Unplanned*, the story about Abby's sudden transformation from Planned Parenthood clinic director to peaceful pro-life activist.

Abby's amazing story made headlines and generated interest for the movie.

I loved being with these three women who continually encouraged me and supported me in this movement. Every day, I had to screw up my courage to approach strangers outside the clinic. I knew I had something to offer them, but I was still a shy little girl inside.

My natural desire to help people in need nudged me toward the women going into the clinic. So many of them looked terrified. Perhaps they were scared about what they were about to do. Even though the group outside the clinic was peaceful, seeing the group may have increased the women's terror.

I realized they faced an agonizing decision. I didn't see them as terrible people. I saw them as girls or women who might need support to keep their babies. Maybe they had been shamed into ending their pregnancies. Maybe they were in desperate financial positions and saw no way to care for another baby. Maybe they were like Tonya, too young to defy their mothers and unaware that there were other options.

If I could be part of helping them see that they had other choices, I could overcome my shyness and stay involved.

One day my friends at the Coalition for Life had a question for me. It surprised me and did not fit my definition of staying involved.

"Claire, would you be willing to share your story of surviving abortion and being adopted with some students from a local Catholic youth group?"

Ohhhh, no, I thought. *How could I do that?*

I could feel my pulse quicken at the mere thought of standing in front of a few young people and talking. As I learned, talking to "some students" meant I would give a talk to some forty or fifty middle and high school students who were participating in a pro-life retreat called Lock-In for Life.

"We've already asked Abby Johnson to speak, and she said she would. We'd love to have you join us too."

"You don't understand," I said, trying to put the conversation in reverse before it went any further. "Do you realize that I'm the world's biggest introvert? And that my biggest fear in life is being up in front of people or being the center of attention?"

At the same time, a small voice somewhere deep inside me said, *Wait a minute. I just may want to do this, if only I can manage to get over my biggest fear.*

I didn't tell them what the voice inside me was saying. I pushed back against their offer.

"Okay," they said. "We understand. But will you think about it?"

"Yes," I said. "I will think about it."

I went home that night and felt a heavy burden weighing on me.

"This is not who I am. I am a behind-the-scenes person, and praying outside the clinic already has me out of my comfort zone," I said out loud to no one. But I couldn't settle on closing that door completely. I determined to tell the Coalition for Life no the following day, and then I spent the next hour trying to suppress the nagging inside me to walk through this open door.

I asked God to make it clear to me if I should do this. Sometimes I pray and already know the answer. This was one of those times. I knew that this opportunity was no accident. It was becoming obvious to me that God was directing my future and moving me one step closer to what he had for me to do.

My activity with the coalition and my growing friendships there inspired me, energized me, fulfilled me, and touched me deeply. With God's help and their support, I knew what my answer would be.

"Okay," I told the coalition people. "I'm ready to share my story."

"Great," they said. "We'll help you figure out how to tell it."

I began preparing for my grand debut, which was scheduled for the first week of December 2009, right before Christmas break.

Anxiety descended on me immediately. *What have I just done? What have I committed myself to?* I was nervous and excited, fearful and hopeful.

I thought I might die of a stage-fright-induced heart attack one second after I was introduced as a speaker, but for now, I was going to fight through my fears as I overprepared in the two weeks before the event.

I believed that God wanted me to do this. Now I was begging him to deliver that extra strength he promised to those who step out and do things they're not sure they want to do in obedience to his will.

But first I had to tell my family.

MY FIRST SPEAKING ENGAGEMENT

For our family, Thanksgiving means much more than a shared meal. Our annual ritual involves driving hours to East Texas, where we spend four days with fifty or more members of Dad's family.

When we all finally gather for Thanksgiving dinner, Dad serves as the unofficial pastor, offering a brief prayer. Dad wanted to preface his prayer of thankfulness that year with an announcement about my origin story. But one of our relatives suggested that the big opening prayer wasn't the best time for dropping a bombshell like mine.

I didn't know it at the time, but our extended family is much like America at large—divided about abortion. We've got pro-lifers and pro-choicers sitting around the same table. But I needed to let them know because, in less than two weeks, I would be telling my story publicly for the first time to the Catholic students. I wanted my family to hear my story before I told it somewhere else. But instead of an announcement to the whole family, I wound up breaking the news to those family members I thought would want to know.

Some couldn't comprehend or believe it. Some rejoiced. Some were silent. Some didn't know exactly how to respond. I get it. Surviving an abortion is a strange thing to wrap your head around. My voice shook the whole time. I hoped I could do a better job when talking to the students.

As I wondered what I could say to the forty or fifty youth who would be waiting for me to deliver something profound or at least interesting, I started creating the talk. Revision after revision followed as I typed away on my laptop.

In a few days, I had a talk that would take the Catholic youth through my journey of finding my birth mother and learning my true origin story. I included the positive sides of being adopted. And I included how grateful I was that my mother's abortion didn't kill me, even though it had come close.

It was time to start practicing. I delivered my talk to an imaginary audience a few times, recording myself on my laptop. Then I watched the recording, made a few changes, and did it again. I kept practicing and revising pretty much until the minute I was introduced. But right before I was to present my talk, I was given some interesting news.

"Claire, small change of plans!" It was Shawn Carney, one of the founders of 40 Days for Life.

"You're speaking to three different groups of Catholic students today, not just one," he told me.

I just stared at Shawn. I was being introduced to the audience at that very moment. My heart was already racing, my palms were sweating, and my name was being announced into a microphone. I breathed deep and told myself, *One step, another step. Just keep walking . . .*

I took the stage. When I looked up, a front row of smiling faces beamed at me. There were my mom and dad and Rachel, some of my new friends from the coalition, and some of my old friends, including Jamie, my best friend from high school who had driven in from Austin, and Bill, my quadriplegic patient. I wanted to please these special people so much and make them proud of me, which probably made me more nervous. But they all looked so pleased before I said even one word that I took another deep breath and relaxed.

Then I dove in. A little over thirty minutes later, I was done. I hadn't died, and the students were actually applauding, some of them enthusiastically. I'm not sure how, but I did it two more times, just like Shawn asked me to. I didn't die then either. In fact, I felt it actually went a little better each time.

When I got back to my apartment that night, I was physically exhausted and emotionally drained. I was also curiously excited about what I had just done.

Okay, I told myself. *That was that!*

9.

MY STORY, MY CALLING

. . .

BUT THAT WASN'T THAT! MORE PEOPLE WERE STARTING to talk about my story—and not only the Catholic girls who heard my first talk. My mom sent copies of my "Abortion, Adoption and Me" flyer to her friends, and I sent a few copies to my friends too.

In January, I received a call from my former high school youth leader. Brandon led the youth group at First Evangelical Free Church of Austin, the church where I grew up.

"Claire, would you be willing to tell your story to your old youth group?" he asked me.

I figured that if I had survived talking to more than one hundred young people I didn't know, it would be easier to talk to twenty or thirty people from my former church. I accepted Brandon's offer. My second speaking engagement would be January 5.

Once the date arrived, I knew I'd been wrong. Surprisingly, I found that talking to people I knew was more emotional and nerve racking than talking to strangers. When I speak to groups I don't know, I'm not as fearful of messing up, because I probably won't see those people again.

But I was going to be talking to students in the same youth

group I'd been in just four years ago. They'd be sitting in the same chairs and in the same room as I had. Some of them would remember me, and some of their parents would be in the audience too. Those parents were still friends with my parents, who would also be there. Would they go up to my parents after I spoke and question them about what I'd said? Many of them didn't know my story and might find it disturbing.

I remembered being a sixteen-year-old in this group and wondered how I could best relate to them, the actual intended audience for my talk. The things I was going to say would be embarrassing for them to hear and for me to say.

When young people hear their youth leader tell them they're going to have a guest speaker talk on abortion, some are skeptical. Others assume the entire talk will be a lecture on three words: *don't have sex!* But sex wasn't the topic of my talk. And I don't ever lecture people. I share my story.

So, I decided to tell a hard story that would also reflect well on who I was and who had raised me. I spoke of hope, redemption, and forgiveness. I talked about the reality of abortion, how it kills babies and hurts the women who turn to it for solutions. And I talked about how I didn't get to choose the circumstances of my birth or my adoption, but I did have choices once I knew my real story, and my choices made a difference in my life.

I chose to forgive and love my birth mother, who had little choice in the decision to abort me. And I chose to boldly embrace who God said I was—his beloved child he had known since before the dawn of time.

"God has something bigger and better in mind for all of us," I told them, "and we can trust him to be with us through the ups and downs of life."

I painted a picture of how God has a purpose for each one of us—a purpose that he determined long before any of us were born. I connected the truth of God having a purpose for each life with the idea that we should be aware of what abortion is and what it does. It ends lives that God made and that God wants to bless and use for his glory.

Then I said something that I knew could make some of the parents in the room uncomfortable. "God loves us so much that even if we go against our parents and what we've been taught or make choices that have consequences, God draws us back to himself. He uses our troubles to show how good and redemptive he is."

With Kleenex and sobs, I made it through my talk. The response from my hometown crowd was warm and positive. If some were upset, they didn't express it. I hope they saw the truth in what I said. I had now survived my second speaking engagement. It turned out it would not be my last.

THREE LONG YEARS

During 2010, my contact with Tonya was infrequent, but we had decided I'd visit her again in December. She later changed the date to January. I was getting ready to leave my apartment and head to the airport when a text showed up on my phone.

"Don't come."

It was from Tonya.

That was the beginning of a long period during which she distanced herself from me, restricting our contact to infrequent texts and phone calls. I'd been sensing a lingering awkwardness in the few communications we did have. She seemed uneasy, cautious. I felt cautious too. I didn't want to say anything that would traumatize her or bring up emotions she wasn't yet ready to revisit.

When I decided I would accept the opportunity to speak to the

Catholic students, I'd asked Tonya whether she was okay with me doing that. She'd said yes, but I wondered whether she now felt more vulnerable than she had anticipated. As my story got out, she was faced with the reactions of her family and friends. I knew she felt guilt and shame, and she had acknowledged to me that she was angry with her mother and the doctor. She didn't know how to handle those feelings, and here I was exposing her story to the world.

It was all part of the strange new reality being written in my life.

A FRIEND FOR LIFE

When I met Abby Johnson, she beamed with kindness and enthusiasm. I was immediately attracted to her that first day I went into the Coalition for Life building. She took me under her wing and encouraged me to learn and grow and become the woman I was meant to be.

Both of us had seen our worlds turned upside down, our identities transformed, and our pro-life passions awoken and empowered. My world was upended when I learned that the birth mother I once thanked for choosing life for me and putting me up for adoption had actually tried to abort me. Abby's world was transformed when she left her position as director of a Planned Parenthood clinic to join forces with the pro-life people praying on the sidewalk.

Other than all that, the two of us couldn't be more different. People say opposites attract, and that was true for us. She's a hard-driving mover and shaker who makes things happen. I'm more of a follower who prefers to let God do the moving and shaking. She's a type A, extroverted personality. I'm a quiet introvert. She's comfortable being a celebrity. She was a public face for the pro-choice movement during her years with Planned Parenthood, and now she is a public face for the pro-life movement and loves speaking to groups—the bigger, the better. But I find being in the public eye uncomfortable. No matter how many times I speak, I never lose the nervousness and stage fright.

We both believe that God brought us together to hold up and strengthen each other in the middle of all the chaos we were going through. Most of the time in the early days of our friendship, Abby was the one holding me up. But I remember one trip we made together where God gave me an opportunity to help Abby.

I attended the March for Life in Washington, DC, and Abby was speaking. Afterward, we went to visit the Holocaust Memorial Museum. We walked through the exhibits and listened to stories of how the Nazis saw Jews as less than human. The evidence of the mass deaths was displayed in glass-enclosed areas, and gruesome photos captured the terrible reality of huge death chambers disguised as shower rooms.

I stood staring at one of the displays and felt a connection to the number of babies lost to abortion. I know it isn't exactly the same, but the loss touched my emotions and held me there. When I turned around, Abby was gone. I looked down the nearby hallways but didn't see her.

"Where are you?" I texted her.

She texted back, "I am in a corner, lying on the floor, and I can't believe what I have done."

I found her and sat with her. She cried and told me that she knew that God forgave her but she couldn't forgive herself and continue to let God use what she had done.

"Abby," I said, "I was that baby, and I love you. Imagine what God can do through your healing to redeem what you have done."

She could hardly grasp what I said. I was like the people she had hurt, yet as an abortion survivor, I didn't look at her as someone with blood on her hands. What I saw when I looked at Abby was a slate wiped clean.

She hugged me and said my words were the most incredible she had ever received. She could go on and believe that she could grow to forgive herself.

That day I knew Abby was both a mentor and a dear friend. And to this day I feel like Abby is someone walking way out in front of me, making her own path in the world and showing me how to find mine. We're both grateful we've been able to encourage and lighten the load for each other as we do our best with the opportunities and platforms that have been given to us.

Abby became a media sensation when she switched sides in the abortion wars, and that media sensation never really died down. She was often traveling and speaking to pro-life groups around the country. One thing Abby didn't have was a high-quality headshot she could send to the people who organized her speaking events. Getting a photo was urgent, they told her. Some people had asked me for my headshot, too, but I didn't have one either.

"Claire, do you want to go with me to Dallas and get your own headshot?" she asked me one day.

We put it on our calendars. During the nearly three-hour drive to the photo studio, both of us laughed so hard that we cried. Abby talks in a very animated way, and she tells the best stories.

We also joked about my possible Indian name. Since Tonya is part Native American and because of the fact that I was born with clubfeet, we decided that my name would be Claire Crooked-Foot.

The drive back was funny too—so funny that we didn't notice the flashing low-fuel light on her dashboard until it was too late. We ran out of gas just as we exited the highway to head for a gas station. Thankfully, some kindly passersby pushed us the rest of the way.

Abby is one of the most organized and detail-oriented people I know, so the fact that she had forgotten to get gas was a hilarious sign of her increasingly chaotic life. It also was one more incident that showed me that people are all so much alike. After I met Abby and found out she was a superstar in the pro-life movement, I looked up to her so much that I didn't imagine we would ever be friends. She was so accomplished and important. Why would she want to hang out with me?

The answer to that question is that people are people no matter whether they're in the public eye or not. We all struggle. We all make mistakes. We all love laughter and desire lives with less pain. And most importantly, we are all loved by our creator. He uses each of us in unique ways. If God had never called me to a public ministry, I know that Abby and I would have still become friends. We love each other for who we are, not for what we do.

A BIG HONOR

I was still getting opportunities to speak here and there, but the invitation I received from some old, old friends was a big, big deal. Every year, Deaconess Pregnancy & Adoption of Oklahoma City hosts a big banquet that raises funds for its operations. When Deaconess asked me to speak at their 2010 banquet, I couldn't say no. This talk would be my chance to thank and bless some of the men and women who helped me when Tonya left me in their care.

Speaking at such an important event would be a big honor and would put me under a lot of pressure. If I bombed this talk, my failure would hurt more than me.

When I was born, Deaconess was a maternity home as well as

an adoption agency. Debbie and others who might be in the audience worked there at the time. Tonya had been staying at the Deaconess home for several weeks before she went into labor. A hospital adjoined the residential part of the facility, so she was taken there for my delivery. Some of the people in the room might be looking at me for the first time as a grown woman—over twenty years after they'd met me as an infant.

The responsibility and the joy of that evening filled me with gratitude for this opportunity to thank all of them for their generosity to me and so many other children and young mothers in difficult circumstances.

Many people assume that those who speak in public give the same basic speech time after time. Maybe some presenters do that, but not me. Each time I have an opportunity to give a talk, I try to figure out how God wants me to tell my story.

This means that one night I might communicate one part of my story so that it connects with people in a powerful way, and on another night I might communicate something else in a new way. At times, these sudden revisions surprise me when I hear them coming out of my own mouth. There are even times when my new way of explaining something triggers tears as the whole range of emotions hits me again.

I don't really speak from a detailed script but rely on a few bullet points to keep me on track. It was becoming clear to me that my notes for the Deaconess talk would contain more bullet points than I'd used before, because they would understand so many details of my story.

I was starting to get more nervous than usual. An anticipated audience of more than five hundred people made this my biggest event ever. Just what I needed: more powerful stage fright!

I would focus on thanking Debbie, who knew more about my life's story than just about anyone. She had worked for months with my mom and dad as they waited for me to arrive, and she had worked with Tonya when she came to place me for adoption. She connected these two worlds, allowing me the good life I've experienced.

Debbie had kept my baby picture on her desk all those years, perhaps anticipating the day when she would no longer need to conceal my unusual origins under a veil of silence.

I knew my talk to my Deaconess family would be emotionally wrenching for me. And I knew I would need to prepare myself to see Debbie, Mom, and Dad together in the audience as I told my story. So I prayed, *Lord, give me strength to get through this!*

"I want to thank everyone here at Deaconess—and especially you, Debbie. All of you opened your arms to me after I miraculously escaped the deathly grip of abortion," I told them through my tears. "Thank you for finding Warren and Barbara Culwell, the parents God wanted for me, the parents who really have loved me more than any parents ever loved a child."

It was a difficult talk, but I survived. Before I knew it, dozens of people were coming up to me, crying, hugging me, thanking me, shaking my hand. People were hugging and thanking Mom too. It was a beautiful evening, and afterward, amid my joy and exhaustion, I found myself asking God, *Lord, is telling people my story my new calling?*

It wasn't long before he answered.

Abby's speaking career was exploding, and she was talking to groups all over the world. Not only was she busy speaking, but she was also working on her book *Unplanned* while being a wife and mom in a family that would eventually include eight kids.

Our friendship was continuing to grow, and I valued her guidance and input. Then one day she asked me a question that startled me. "Claire, would you like to speak to more groups about your own story? I can recommend you to all the groups I speak to so that maybe you can speak to them next."

Her offer turned me into an immediate nervous wreck. I was certain that just about anyone else could be a better speaker than I could, but I was the best person to tell my own story. I looked at Abby's smiling face. She seemed about to say, "Great! I knew you would." She put her hand on my arm, ready to give a supportive pat.

I silently battled fear. I didn't want to disappoint Abby or God. I also knew I needed to make this decision based on something other than my emotions. It was obvious that opportunities were coming my way that I had not sought out. I really was content to stay in the background of this pro-life movement. But I didn't want fear to determine what I should do.

Finally I said, "I'm willing to give it a try, but I know, if this doesn't work, God will shut the door, and I'm totally okay with that."

Some people will promise you their support but won't back up that promise with action. Abby immediately got involved in turning me into the best speaker possible. She gave me an education on what public speaking was all about.

"It's not just information," she told me. "You need to move people if you want them to really hear you. And you need to encourage people to take action, not just hear your story and walk away unaffected."

Abby was right there with me the next couple of times I shared my story. As I spoke, she gave me encouraging looks. And afterward, she offered advice and constructive criticism, which I gladly received. At the same time, I learned to tell my story by hearing Abby tell hers. Listening to her, I got an education not only on how to speak but also on how to articulate my growing passion for the pro-life movement.

Abby also introduced me to her agent, Wes Yoder, who started a company called Ambassador Speakers Bureau in Nashville more than twenty years earlier. When people want to book speakers like Rick Warren of Saddleback Church, Jim Daly of Focus on the Family, Ruth Graham, Abby Johnson, and more than two hundred others, they contact Ambassador.

Signing with an agent was exciting but scary. It felt like I was walking away from the nursing career that had been my goal for years, because speaking engagements required that I be available to travel. And I didn't really have a clear picture of what I was walking toward.

But sure enough, more speaking opportunities came my way, which gave me chances to experience stage fright on a more regular basis. I'm still an introvert. I still get nervous when I talk publicly. I need to pray as I'm onstage to keep myself standing upright and to know what to say.

And I still find myself asking God, *Why me? Are you sure you want the most introverted person who ever existed to keep speaking publicly about the most controversial topic of our time?* So far the answer seems to be yes. And as I began telling my story more, I slowly became more comfortable telling it.

Thanks to Abby's friendship and endorsement, I began meeting everyone who's anyone in the pro-life movement. Three such people had a powerful impact on my life and my thinking about abortion.

Gianna Jessen is a fellow abortion survivor whose story was told in a book (*Gianna: Aborted, and Lived to Tell About It*) and a movie (*October Baby*).[1] She survived a saline abortion, a grisly process that involves injecting a chemical solution into the uterus, inducing uterine contractions that expel the child. She was born two months premature and with cerebral palsy, which she describes as a "tremendous gift."[2]

Gianna has testified before political leaders around the world, saying, "If abortion is about women's rights, then what were mine?"[3] She was present in the White House in 2002 when President George W. Bush signed into law the Born-Alive Infants Protection Act, and Mother Teresa praised her pro-life work.

I had read Gianna's book after I met her on the sidewalk across from my student apartment in College Station. Later I was able to hear her speak and share her moving story.

Lila Rose is best known for her undercover videos that expose the dark underside of the abortion industry. Many people think of abortion as a simple medical procedure, but Lila's videos have exposed Planned Parenthood's brutality and lack of morality. She was fifteen years old when she founded the organization Live Action, "one of the leading national pro-life and human rights organizations in America, dedicated to ending abortion and inspiring a culture that respects and defends life."[4] In 2014, *Christianity Today* featured her among young leaders in its article "33 under 33."[5]

When I met Lila, I was amazed at her energy and assertiveness. Her example encouraged me to think about what I could do to use my own skills and perspectives to tell more people the truth about abortion.

Being around Gianna and Lila also showed me that I didn't need to be down on myself for being young. They had both started

Barbara and Warren met at a Campus Crusade conference and enjoy doing ministry together as a couple.

Barbara shared with their ministry partners her journey of waiting for God's timing for a baby.

WAIT WAIT wait ...

May 8,1987

Dear Friend,

WAITING isn't fun is it? It's hard because you don't know the outcome of what you're **waiting** for. You don't really know if it will ever happen. It's hard to know exactly how to pray. It's easy to wonder if God really cares it's taking so long. It's hard to know how to plan. **Waiting.**

Warren and I have been **waiting** for the Lord to give us a child for almost three years now. It might not seem like that long, but I doubt that a day has gone by that we haven't thought about it in some way. The Lord has taught both of us so much as we have **waited.**

> "I would have despaired unless I had believed
> that I would see the goodness of the Lord in
> the land of the living.
> Wait for the Lord;
> Be strong, and let your heart take courage;
> Yes, wait for the Lord."
> Ps. 27:13-14

In the midst of many disappointing times, I have chosen to focus on God's goodness. We have done test after test; written many checks; waited for doctor's appointments and test results; watched many friends bring home their babies; and shed many tears. I think I really would have despaired if I had not believed that God cared about me. This time of **waiting** has helped me to see that throughout Scripture God talks about His love for His children and that His plans for us are good. I may not understand His plan, but I know that He knows what is best for us. I am thankful for what the Lord has taught me during this time, because I realize that it's more important that I know and understand the Lord than to get what I want when I want it.

In the fall we started to apply for adoption at an agency in Oklahoma. We were encouraged to find this agency because they want adoptive parents who will raise their children in a Christian environment. Once you have been approved, they say a child could be placed in your home anywhere from 2 weeks to probably sometime within a year. We seemed hopeful that maybe someday we would actually have a child! We started the application process and the **waiting** has started again. Each step has taken longer than we anticipated, but we know it is still quicker than some agencies. We have had to do a home study with an agency in our home state. When we thought we were almost ready to be approved, our social worker said that she didn't think we were quite ready because there are some issue regarding infertility and adoption that we still needed to work through. She thinks this should take 3-6 months. We have had a hard time communicating with her and feeling understood. Today we met with her again and with her supervisor, but we still didn't feel understood. So, we are still **waiting** to get the issues worked out. We look forward to getting our final approval, and then we will wait for our phone call indicating it's time to go get our baby!

Please pray for us that we would "be strong, and let our hearts take courage." We know that the Lord's timing is perfect and that he has the baby picked out for us that He wants us to have. It's still not fun to wait!

We love you!

Warren and Barbara Culwell
4324 Stanford Dallas, Tx. 75225 214-368-8865
Campus Crusade for Christ

Barbara and Warren wrote letters of gratitude to my birth mother for the agency to give to her.

> May 3, 1988
>
> Dear Birthmother,
>
> I can't believe this time has finally come! My husband & I have longed to have a child for almost 4 years now. Of course, like most couples starting a family we didn't think we would have any trouble, but things didn't go as we planned. We went through many tests, shed many tears, & wondered what the Lord was trying to do. Through all of this, our desire for children has grown even deeper, especially as we have watched most of our friends & family have children. Finally, we realized we might not be able to conceive a child of our own, so we started to pursue adoption because we couldn't imagine going through life without children. We soon came across Deaconess Home & were excited about how they did things. Our whole adoption process has taken a little longer than we thought — but we always knew there must be some reason that God had a special baby for us & it just wasn't time yet.
>
> On March 7th we got a call about your baby. We were so excited — but unsure

> Dear Special Friend,
>
> I've been waiting to write to you for two months and tell you how I've prayed for you and your baby girl...

Debbie Campbell, the case-worker for my adoption, and Betty Hollingsworth, the former director of Deaconess Pregnancy and Adoption, held me one last time before giving me to Warren and Barbara.

Barbara and Warren were thrilled to announce their newborn little girl!

Once upon a time (March 6, 1988 to be exact), a little bitty baby girl was born. She was so tiny (3 lbs. 2 oz.) because she was born 10 weeks early. The next day, a couple in Dallas, Warren and Barbara Culwell got a phone call saying this could be the baby God had for them. They were so excited because they had been wanting a baby for a long, long, time. They also were a little apprehensive because they were unsure of how things would work out. Over the next 8 weeks as the little girl got bigger and stronger, Warren and Barbara asked lots of questions, prayed alot, and talked to several doctors.

During a walk in the neighborhood, Warren and Barbara were grateful to meet Dr. James Roach, who played an essential role in my recovery from the complications of my premature birth.

This Radio Flyer wagon was transformed into a traction bed as I received treatment for my dislocated hip.

I was dressed in my Easter Sunday best to travel with my mom and dad to meet my new sister, Rachel.

We gathered together for a photo at our 1998 Thanksgiving family reunion in Texas (Rachel on left, me on right).

Barbara and I posed for a picture near the stop sign I grabbed when trying to avoid going to school in Costa Rica.

Ministry in Mexico meant adjusting to a different home and culture.

I finally got to meet my birth mother in Dallas in 2009. After hugging and saying hello, we exchanged gifts.

I had no plans to become a speaker when my mom and I put together this flyer. I gave it to the people who prayed in front of the Planned Parenthood clinic near my student apartment in College Station.

Abortion, *Adoption* and Me

In March of 2009, (when I was 21 years old), I met the most beautiful woman I had ever seen- not because she had a perfect appearance or wore fancy things- but because she is my **birth mother**. She gave me life. She gave me the most wonderful **family**. She thought about my **future** instead of her own. She was **selfless**. She gave me the best gift I've ever been given and that's the gift of life. I will always love her for that and I thought "no one will ever give me a gift like that again!"

...Not flesh of my flesh...but heart of my heart...

I was **adopted** at birth by a couple who desperately wanted kids but couldn't have their own. My dad, Warren, is the wisest, most stable, solid provider in the world. My mom, Barbara, is the most caring, sincere, loving mother I know. My sister, Rachel, is fun, sweet and I wouldn't trade her for any other sister! I am very blessed.

My family Barbara, Warren, me and Rachel

In May of 2009, I visited the hometown of my birth mother (Tonya) in Oklahoma. I met her other daughters (my half sisters) and it was an amazing experience to see what it would have been like to grow up where I was born. I had no idea that **what she was going to tell me that day would change my life forever.** After thanking her for choosing to give me life, she broke down into tears.

She told me that at 14 years old, she went to an abortion clinic to have an abortion because she didn't ... ns. Back then, they didn't do sonograms. Because of that, a couple months later, nant and went back to the abortion clinic. It was too late to get another that she had been pregnant with twins.

Due to a generous donation from some of our friends, Sanctuary of Hope planted three trees honoring me, my parents, and my birth mother.

Celebration! Pastor John Hagee's dream of building a home for mothers facing unwanted pregnancies became a reality. Pictured at the groundbreaking are (left to right) Kendal and Matt Hagee; Warren, Barbara, and me; and Diana and John Hagee.

Tony Perkins, president of the Family Research Council, interviewed me and abortion survivors Josiah Presley and Melissa Ohden at FRC's 2019 Values Voter Summit in DC.

Female members of the North Carolina legislature joined fellow abortion survivor Gianna Jessen (in green dress) and me at a press conference on the Born-Alive Abortion Survivors Protection Act.

Discussion of SB 9 (Sen. Castlen)
AN ACT RELATING TO ABORTION AND DECLARING AN EMERGENCY

I testified in favor of Senate Bill 9, the Heartbeat Bill, before the Kentucky senate.

Alive from New York brought a crowd to Times Square for a powerful pro-life event that was streamed worldwide. Shown (left to right) are Jim Daly, president of Focus on the Family; abortion survivors Melissa Ohden and Josiah Presley; me; and Jeanne Mancini, the president of March for Life.

The morning after Alive from New York, Abby Johnson and I appeared in a Fox News segment.

David and I welcomed Sadie June into our big family in early 2013.

My father
officiated
our wedding.

Our kids were
a big part of
our wedding
celebration.

Every year we gather together in East Texas for Christmas
with lots of our family. This photo is from 2019.

speaking out when they were younger than I was, and they were able to have a tremendous impact on people despite their youth.

Joe Pojman is the founder and executive director of the Texas Alliance for Life, which works to protect innocent human life through peaceful and legal means. For more than thirty years, Joe has lobbied the Texas legislature about major pro-life bills. His work has been successful, as Texas has passed laws covering parental notice and consent, the Prenatal Protection Act, the sonogram bill, the Choose Life license plate bill, and a bill to defund Planned Parenthood across the state.[6]

I was not a very political person when I met Joe, but he showed me how beliefs and values about life issues can be turned into action that saves lives.

The more I interacted with pro-life leaders like Gianna, Lila, and Joe, the more I learned about people and experiences that were different from my own. They broadened my perspective, deepened my commitment and helped me see the variety and depth of the nationwide pro-life movement. I deeply valued encouragement from those who had been part of the movement much longer than I had. These friends also gave me the tips and coaching I needed to grow in my speaking skills.

NEW OPPORTUNITIES, INTERNATIONAL REACH

One thing led to another as I traveled and spoke more across the country. I made the difficult decision to stop my nursing studies altogether. Until then, I had been trying to speak and take classes. So I left Blinn College and College Station and moved back to Austin to be near my family.

I was busy, but nothing like Abby. Then I received a surprising call from Ambassador Speakers. Was I familiar with *The 700 Club,* the Christian news and entertainment program started by Pat Robertson way back in 1966? They wanted to feature me as a guest on the show. Would it be okay if they sent a film crew to Austin the next week?

It was the latest in a series of offers I was receiving to reach larger and larger audiences. And even though I suspected that I would be as nervous in front of television cameras as I was in front of crowds of people, I saw it as a wonderful opportunity to tell my story and change hearts and minds. I said yes.

The program featuring me aired on January 7, 2011. That's when things really began to explode in my speaking career. Ambassador was getting more and more requests for me. One day I would be at a Wisconsin Right to Life rally. The next day I would be the guest of the Catholic Diocese of Little Rock, Arkansas. The next week I would be at a University of San Diego Students for Life meeting.

The events came one after another, all across the country: the Living Alternatives Pregnancy Resource Center in Kokomo, Indiana; a student group at King University in Bristol, Tennessee; Seacoast Church in Greensboro, North Carolina; Hannah's Home for unplanned pregnancies in Mentor, Ohio; Bear Catholic Campus Ministry in Greeley, Colorado.

There were Lutheran churches, Baptist churches, Methodist churches, Catholic churches, Bible churches, Evangelical Free churches, and all kinds of independent evangelical churches. I even spoke at a Campus Crusade event for teen moms in Denver.

And the requests came from international organizations as well. Soon I was a true globe-trotting frequent flier, speaking for the Alliance for Life Ontario in Canada, the Pro Life Campaign and the Lumen Fidei Institute in Ireland, and a meeting of Family Life International in New Zealand.

Now that I was speaking to so many different groups, I was constantly changing the way I told my story. New events were happening in my life, I was gaining new perspectives through my friendship with pro-life leaders, and I had started talking once again with Tonya. All these developments affected what I said and how I said it.

Day by day, step by step, it seemed God was paving a pathway for me that I could follow. His hand was on my life, and I prayed that his love and grace would shine through the words I spoke.

But I wasn't the only one going through tremendous change. My old College Station neighborhood was changing as well and would continue to do so for years: 40 Days for Life would continue to expand its national and international outreach. Then in 2013, the Planned Parenthood clinic would close down. By 2015, the building had been purchased and repurposed by a pro-life pregnancy center.

"What was once a place of death and grief where an estimated 6,400 abortions were performed has been transformed into a place of life," said Tracy Frank, the executive director of Hope Pregnancy Centers. "We feel like we have reclaimed and redeemed the ground."[7]

Since then, other spaces where abortions once took place have been converted into pro-life clinics for women seeking better alternatives. In 2020, the Christian magazine *World* reported on some of these transformations:

Austin and Bryan, Texas. Chattanooga, Tenn. Elkton, Md. Grand Rapids, Mich. Toledo, Ohio. Wichita, Kan. These are seven of the at least 20 cities where pro-life groups have

taken over and repurposed former surgical abortion facilities. They are now crisis pregnancy centers, pro-life offices,
or memorials.[8]

I'm not a big fan of this kind of conversion process. I don't like
the idea of putting millions of dollars into the abortion industry's
budget by purchasing their old buildings. But I understand why
others support it.

I still miss the old neighborhood. And I will never forget the
transformations—big and small—that took place there.

10.

MY PERSONAL
"UNPLANNED"

. . .

"**I**'VE GOT TO DO THIS RIGHT NOW!" I ANNOUNCED TO MYself early one morning as I threw on some clothes and rushed out the door to the nearest Walgreens pharmacy.

It was June 2012, and I was in full crisis mode. A few days earlier, I had started experiencing what seemed to be morning sickness. I had also missed a number of periods. I'd been attributing that to a really stressful schedule and other emotions that had begun to overwhelm me.

Was I pregnant? I already sensed that I was, but I wasn't sure. I desperately needed to know right away. I located a pregnancy test and took it to the cash register, trembling and breathing rapidly as I pulled out some cash. I didn't want to use a credit card with my name on it. That small choice revealed my feelings of shame. I was unmarried.

David, the father of my baby, was waiting in the car outside the pharmacy. He had driven me to get the pregnancy test and had assured me that we would be fine. He loved me and supported me, and we would go through this together.

As the clerk handed me my change, I gave her a weak smile. I wondered whether she could see customers' anxiety when they bought pregnancy tests. I imagined that women who were eager to be pregnant felt a very different kind of anxiety.

I took my package back to the restroom inside the Walgreens and did the test there. I couldn't even wait to take it back home. I peed in the little plastic cup, dipped the test stick into the liquid, and waited to see the result. The seconds seemed like minutes or hours as my mind played the what-if game.

What if I'm not pregnant? Phew! Then I can thank God, go home, and get on with my life.

What if I am pregnant? I would still thank God because I've always wanted to be a mother and I truly value every life, including the new one that might be growing inside me.

But it seemed that everything I would face if I were pregnant would be difficult and messy. My whole family would be disappointed with me for failing to live up to the morals they had taught me, the morals that I professed and lived out, at least most of the time.

Then there was my speaking ministry. I had events booked through the next eight months. Would these churches, student groups, and pregnancy centers still welcome a pro-life speaker who was pregnant outside marriage? I hoped they would but feared they wouldn't.

My ministry will be over.

Sure enough, the test turned colors. I was pregnant, according to a test that claimed to be accurate 99 percent of the time.

I thought back to how I got here.

HOW IT ALL BEGAN

About a year earlier, I boarded a plane from Orlando, Florida, to go back home to Austin. I had gone to Orlando to recover from the shock of Tonya abruptly canceling our planned meeting. I had been doing what I could to build a bridge to her, forgive her, and love her, but it seemed like all I received from her was rejection.

Tonya's rejection had stirred up a number of emotions as I tried to navigate my own rapidly changing life. I understood that she had a lot to process and may have needed time to work through those things, but it still hurt.

In Orlando, I spent time with friends and tried to relax. I went with them to Disney World, thinking that "the happiest place on earth" would heal my emotional wounds. The visit was fun, a breather from my complicated life back home. But the results were temporary.

As I took my seat on the airplane, I found myself next to an attractive young man who had his nose buried in a book, Joel Osteen's *Your Best Life Now.* We said hello, then asked each other why and where we were traveling. That led to complicated answers for both of us. Before long, we were sharing our life stories. I assumed my story would be more dramatic until David started telling his.

David had been adopted, but his experience was the opposite of mine. He didn't learn of his adoption until he was thirteen. He shared openly how that sudden revelation was traumatic, leading to a period of confusion and rebellion. Now, a single dad of three children he loved dearly, David was picking up the pieces of a messy life and trying to make changes that would create stability for his family.

His story touched me deeply. I saw a good man courageously trying to take care of his children in a situation so many other men walked away from. Even though he wasn't married, he took his responsibility to his three young children (at the time they were one and a half, three, and eight years old) seriously and was extremely involved in their lives.

His story of his adoption and his intentional rebuilding of his life after making poor choices connected with my desire to help others who were suffering. And my story of my mixed emotions connected with his kind and generous spirit.

As our flight began its descent into Austin, we exchanged contact information and agreed to talk soon. Of course, I wondered whether he really would call. He did. We went on our first date and then another one and another, and pretty soon our relationship deepened.

We became intimate as I sought to fill the emotional vulnerabilities in my life with the love of a man. I was at a broken place in my life. I knew what was true and good and healthy. I knew what would have been the right decision as our relationship grew. But my emotions clouded our choices. I'd also become close to David's children. I loved them too.

I wasn't admitting to myself what was happening and that I needed comfort. My schedule continued to grow more frantic with so many opportunities to speak. Life was a whirlwind.

WHAT NEXT?

Internally I struggled. My conscience told me, *I am someone people put on a pedestal. I am on a stage talking about what God says is true, yet I am living by my emotions and not living out my faith. I am talking about purity. I am now the woman I have been speaking to!*

I walked out of the pharmacy after taking the pregnancy test. David was standing by the car and pulled me into a warm embrace as I nodded. "Yes," I finally said.

He was true to his word and encouraged me that we would continue our relationship and have this baby. He knew I would never consider an abortion, and he felt the same way. Even though the pregnancy test claimed to be 99 percent accurate, the directions on the box told me to confirm that I was actually pregnant. I knew what I needed to do next.

David and I headed for a nearby pregnancy center operated by a pro-life group in Austin. In my crisis mode, I needed confirmation of my pregnancy before I could think of how to move forward. The pregnancy center seemed a logical place to go. I had referred many pregnant women there and had spoken at fundraising banquets for many similar centers.

I knew the people there would give me personal attention and loving care, but I was worried. Even though I had no official position with any organization, I was a somewhat public person and visible representative of the pro-life movement. I was intricately involved with a number of ministries and clinics. Some might even consider me a kind of leader. And I knew what the New Testament said about leaders; they are held to a higher standard.

How would my fellow pro-life activists respond to my unplanned pregnancy? Even more importantly, would the people working at the center recognize me? Would they know about my ministry speaking to pro-life groups? If they knew, would they grant me the privacy they promised any other patient, or would they whisper and turn my story into a scandal?

If people were going to find out that I was pregnant, I wanted them to hear it from me, not from someone whose whispers could sink my ministry. I needed the chance to be living proof of the message I had been proclaiming: preserve the life of the baby, even if the circumstances are difficult.

I arrived at the center tense, sweating profusely, and still in full crisis mode. It turned out that a couple of the people at the clinic did recognize me from my flyer. They greeted me warmly and seemed so pleased to have a pro-life speaker come through their doors. Maybe they thought I was there as a representative for the pro-life movement. While I was certainly pro-life, that was not my purpose that day.

I told them I thought I was pregnant and wanted an ultrasound to make sure the test result was correct. "I need to make sure that you please don't tell anyone about this until I have a chance to talk to everyone myself," I pleaded with the clinic workers, asking them to talk me down off of this psychological ledge.

They assured me of their silence. And then they did what I'd known they would do. They sat with me and listened as I poured out my anxiety. Their love and understanding were a balm to my soul. They talked about taking one step at a time, beginning with calming down before getting the ultrasound.

I can't express how wonderful it was to be encouraged to slow down. I'd been on unstable ground for so long that I grabbed on to those moments of rest. We were only sitting on a comfortable couch in a small room, but it felt like a slice of heaven—kind women, deep breaths, a cool glass of water, and the touch of a hand on my trembling fingers. I relaxed. In a few moments, I was ready to see whether I carried a life inside me.

I was led into the room with the ultrasound machine. I lay on the table while the technician squirted gel on my tummy. The screen of the machine was placed so I could see it; then the technician turned it on and took the wand in her hand. The smooth, rounded surface of the instrument slid easily over my gelled stomach. Grainy images appeared on the screen.

I'd seen a lot of ultrasounds and knew it could take a little while for images to come into focus. Then I heard it. The soft, rhythmic beating of my baby's tiny heart. An image came onto the screen. I was looking at my beautiful child.

MY FIRST PHONE CALL

"Abby, it's Claire," I said into my phone, competing with a lot of background noise. "Abby, what's going on?"

She calmly informed me that she was in the hospital about to deliver her second child, then asked what was going on with me. I quickly unpacked my crisis for her, sharing my fears about how people would react once they knew about my secret sin.

"You need to stop apologizing about this right now," Abby told me. "Having sex with your boyfriend may be sinful, but there is nothing sinful about the beautiful life you carry inside you."

I cried as Abby spoke to the shame I felt deep in my soul.

"Claire, you need to stop with all the negativity and hold your head high," she said. "You need to be proud of the life you carry within you."

As the background noises grew louder, Abby promised to stand with me and walk with me every step of the way. Before saying goodbye, she offered me one additional nugget of wisdom.

"How you talk about your pregnancy is going to influence how other people will talk about your pregnancy," she said. "You need to show how this child is a good and joyful thing, not a sin or a source of dread and anxiety."

This was just the advice I desperately needed before having

some of the most difficult conversations of my life with the people that meant the most to me. I knew God had forgiven me and accepted me, and Abby had been more than gracious. But frankly, I was a bit worried about how Mom and Dad would react to my news.

As I was growing up, they met my occasional outbursts of misbehavior with sorrow and disappointment. In fact, disappointing them was so disturbing to me that my desire to not let them down was much more effective at preventing misbehavior than a million spankings or groundings ever would have been. Now I needed to let them know about something that would gravely upset them. No one in our family had ever faced a problem like this.

Abby had asked me a question during our brief phone call: "So, what's the worst that could happen?"

"Well, for one thing, my entire speaking ministry is going to disappear," I told her. "For another thing, I'll have to live with the knowledge of how much this will hurt my parents." But I knew I needed to do this, so David and I decided to meet my parents for dinner. As we walked into the restaurant, I wondered why I had suggested having a meal together. I felt like I would throw up whatever I ate. This telling would be the hardest.

I wasn't afraid that my parents would be mad or unkind. Quite the opposite. I had already disappointed them by being in a serious relationship with a divorced man. David was older than me. He had battle scars from his former life, and my parents had hoped I'd end up with a young man without that many traumas. They wanted me to heal from my own discovery about my birth and not complicate my life with another person who needed healing. Even so, they accepted David and continued to be the loving parents they'd always been.

I was dreading this meeting because I knew that what I had done and what lay ahead for me would turn their worlds upside down too. They were leaders in their Christian community who had raised their girls in the most loving and godly way they could. They gave unconditional, selfless love to us and everyone they met. And my life situation would now reflect on them. It was unfair, but it would happen. They'd never taught us that Christians never make mistakes, never sin, always make the best choices. Never! But that wouldn't change the difficulty of seeing their adult child face a bumpy road.

One of the biggest challenges for many Christians is dealing with the reality that we are all flawed people. Not one of us is perfect. When we make mistakes, we prefer to take them privately to the Lord with our sincere repentance and experience his love and forgiveness. That's an essential and wonderful part of a personal relationship with Jesus. But if that mistake becomes public, some believers are not so loving and forgiving. It may become very painful to endure the judgment that often comes as a result.

My parents are an exception. They are not judgmental. But I knew they would be hurt by the consequences I would experience, and I knew they might also face unkind judgments.

We all sat down and ordered our meal. I pulled a gift bag out of my purse and put it in front of me on the table. "I have something to tell you. I'm really nervous and sick to my stomach because I know this is going to be a disappointment and hard for our family. But I'm also excited because God always has a plan, and I'm trusting him, and I know you are too. We found out that I'm pregnant. You are going to be grandparents."

I handed them the gift bag and watched them open a framed photo of my ultrasound. I didn't give them time to say anything but went on to tell them that David and I hadn't had time to talk through any plans.

As they looked at the ultrasound, they responded as I had expected. They said they loved me and supported me and would be with me throughout all of what was ahead. I knew, though, that they were heartbroken. They had not gotten to make a pregnancy announcement of their own, and they would not be making this one the way they would have hoped.

This was their first grandbaby, and I knew they would have loved to go home and start calling friends to tell them the wonderful news. Now that wonderful news was mixed with painful emotions.

We left the restaurant, and I knew that, no matter what, my parents would support me.

Now we needed to tell other people. Not everyone was so positive. Some family members and friends were shocked, while others brushed it off. Many offered me free advice. One family member suggested I get an abortion, an act I would never consider for a split second. Being a mother was something I had dreamed of since I was a little girl. And my words about saving babies' lives were heartfelt. I would never choose an abortion. Another suggested I place my child for adoption.

Some suggested that David and I quickly marry and pretend the pregnancy began while we were married. But I wanted to be honest about what was going on, not change the truth in an effort to save my pride or my ministry.

Before hearing these suggestions, I had never thought of my pregnancy as a problem to be solved. But solving my "problem" was the main focus for some of my family and friends. The whole experience helped me understand and identify with Tonya even more than I had already. I thought about all she had been through with her unplanned pregnancy, all the shame she had endured, all the pressure to abort me and my twin.

As I came to terms with a pregnancy I had never sought, I saw how my behavior was affecting everyone I loved. All these conversations had been difficult, but my next phone call worried me even more. I needed to call my agents, Wes and Gloria. They had already booked me for some twenty speaking engagements over the next eight months. I wanted to tell them about my significant new life event and see what they thought we should do.

"Well," Wes said, laughing, "at least you're being up front and telling us about your change as opposed to letting us find out about it ourselves, as some of our other speakers have done!"

We talked for a bit before finally agreeing on a plan. They would call all twenty of the groups that had booked me, explain the situation, and give them the option to cancel me if that's what they wanted to do.

"These groups need to know," Gloria said, "and they need to have the option to change their minds about booking you based on this new information."

This would be my chance to see how churches and other Christian organizations treated me now that I had failed to live up to the beliefs and values we shared about sexuality. While I hoped most would give me the chance to tell my story, I worried that most would cancel me.

A week later, Gloria gave me the update. As it turned out, half the groups canceled me and requested another speaker, while the other half kept me on their schedules.

Gloria handled everything with grace and professionalism, but the whole process left me feeling awkward and shameful. It became a lonely time for me, as it seemed many people were willing to offer advice or judgment but few were willing to reach out to me and comfort me. Aside from Abby, my parents, and a few of my parents' friends from Campus Crusade, everyone kept their distance, including most of my friends in the pro-life movement.

WELCOMING SADIE JUNE

When I was about twenty weeks pregnant, I visited my obstetrician-gynecologist so I could have another ultrasound and see whether I was carrying a girl or a boy.

"It's a girl!" he told me.

I was so happy I cried.

Unfortunately, I soon experienced extreme morning sickness that hospitalized me for ten days. But I eventually recovered, and thankfully the rest of my pregnancy was uneventful. As my due date grew near, I knew I wanted to have Sadie June naturally so my mom and David could be in the room for the delivery. The doctors told me it was likely that I would need to have a cesarean section because of my former hip issues.

After months of waiting, my water broke. When I'd been in labor for twelve hours, the doctors said they would need to perform a C-section after all. David and my mom put on sterile gowns and masks. If all went well, they would allow David to be with me until they got the baby out. Then he would take Sadie June to the nursery, and my mom would stay in recovery with me.

But all did not go well. I had been given an epidural that was intended to completely numb the lower half of my body but allow me to be awake for the delivery. The epidural didn't work. I started feeling the pain of the surgery as things began to move rapidly. The doctor pulled Sadie June out and handed her to David. He put her next to me, so I could see her. I couldn't hold her then because

I was still being administered drugs, so David took her to the NICU. My parents were right next to him, getting their own first glimpse of their first grandchild.

After I was taken to the recovery room, David placed Sadie June in my arms for the first time. I just gazed at this miracle of life with an all-consuming joy. The next people to hold her were my parents who were standing right next to us. The looks on their faces said it all: love beyond words.

The three days I spent in the hospital after Sadie June's birth were a whirlwind of joy and sleeplessness. I was utterly exhausted when a final visitor entered my room, but I perked up when I heard a familiar and comforting voice from my childhood. It was Mrs. Dodds, our family friend from Costa Rica. My relationship with her was one of my most valued in the world.

As she sat in a rocking chair across the room from me, holding Sadie June, she looked up at me with the most loving, tender eyes and told me something that has stayed with me ever since.

"Claire," she said, "God's just not done writing your story, and Sadie June is the next chapter."

REUNITED AGAIN

Sure enough, I loved being a mother, even more than I'd thought I would. Over time I had become increasingly pro-life without ever having given birth myself. Now being a mother and holding my own child brought a whole new depth to my passion for preserving and valuing all life.

I embraced Sadie June's birth as a blessing. Her life was yet another miracle in my miracle-filled story. Now there were two people who wouldn't be alive if an abortion had ended my life.

When everything was said and done, my unplanned pregnancy actually brought my whole family together. My parents love David and the kids, whom I now love as children of my own, the same way my parents chose and loved me. And somehow, having a child of my own had a powerful effect on my relationship with Tonya.

I had called her when I found out I was pregnant. She was thrilled! I think she identified with me in a way she hadn't before. I had seemed to have this perfect life and make a series of wise choices, not like the life she had lived. Now I was unmarried and pregnant . . . different circumstances but the same outcome. The distancing ended, and we stayed in touch more often.

We talked about connecting so Tonya could meet her granddaughter. I had a speaking engagement in Tulsa when Sadie June was about ten months old. Tonya and her daughters decided to drive to Tulsa so they could all meet the newest addition to their family.

I arrived at the restaurant ahead of Tonya and her daughters and sat down with Sadie June in my arms. I saw them walk in and was once again struck by how much Tonya looks and acts like me. A new grandmother might hurry over to see the baby, but Tonya slowly made her way over to the table. She was beaming, excited, happy.

I stood up to place Sadie June in Tonya's outstretched arms. Our eyes met, and the glistening tears in her eyes were tears of joy. Our smiles widened as Tonya held her granddaughter close to her heart. She shook her head slightly with a sense of amazement that her trauma had ended with the redemption of the woman in front of her and the baby in her arms.

That moment was the beginning of a growing and sustained relationship with Tonya.

WEDDING BELLS

Most people thought David and I would get married right after finding out I was pregnant. We didn't. We didn't want the outside pressure to get married to be the reason we made that commitment.

The two of us had already been through a lot together in the past few months. David had uprooted his three children and moved to Texas. Then came my pregnancy, followed immediately by the sudden disappearance of most of my speaking ministry. Then beautiful Sadie June came into our lives.

Planning and organizing a public wedding was more than we felt we could navigate at the time. So David and I exchanged private vows with each other, and then we quickly focused all our energy on creating the best possible home for our new family of six.

The formal wedding took place on April 9, 2016. Dad did double duty: walking me down the aisle and then officiating at the outdoor ceremony full of Scripture and prayer before one hundred or so family and friends.

The months before the ceremony had been a time of forgiveness and healing for my family members and me. Mom and Dad and I were able to talk about the ways we had hurt one another over the years and forgive one another, creating a clean slate for all.

As David and I and our families prayed together before the ceremony, I could sense the powerful love that flowed among us all. The ceremony itself was much more than a mere formality, as David and I reaffirmed our vows and recommitted ourselves to loving each other and serving our children. As far as I could tell, there wasn't a dry eye among us.

David was overwhelmed. "That whole day was packed so full

of emotions," he admitted to me later. "But standing there and praying together was the most surreal for me."

We had put our families through trials and tribulations, and for a while, our relationships were awkward. But now all of that was behind us, healed and forgiven. The evidence was the grace everyone showed.

David told my dad how he was so excited to finally have a wedding where he could say "I do" and formally make me his wife in front of our kids and all the people who had meant so much to us. He was so thankful that God had brought us to this point.

There was also a sweet time of prayer during the ceremony with David and me, all the kids, and our parents. Then Mom and Dad gave each of the kids a Bible with his or her name monogrammed on the cover. "This is God's good word for you," Dad told them. "Knowing him and centering your life on what he says in this book is the best way you can live your life. He is good and has good plans for each of you."

My friend Heather sang the worship song "Good Good Father" written by Chris Tomlin. It was true. Our heavenly Father had been so very good to us. Despite moments of rebellion and chaos, our broken relationships, and our shortcomings, God had brought us together.

He had knit together the pieces of us longing for lasting relationship, grace, forgiveness, redemption, and peace, and he had given us each other. I was gifted some of the most incredible things that day: to be a wife to my best friend, to be a mom to our four children, to be forgiven and seen in a new light by our family and friends, to be walked down the aisle and married by my daddy, and to begin a journey of a lifetime.

II.

TURNING ASHES
INTO BEAUTY

. . .

I HAD JUST WALKED OFF THE STAGE TO GREET PEOPLE from the audience. I saw her coming and knew by the look in her eyes that she had had an abortion.

"My name is Susan." Her soft voice trembled as tears streamed down her face. She managed a shy smile and shrugged as if a heavy weight had been lifted.

I took her extended hand in both of mine and pulled her in for a hug. She went on to tell me her story. "I've never told anyone what I did almost twenty years ago, and when I came here tonight, I didn't plan on telling anyone either. But when you shared about meeting your birth mother and forgiving her and then you said that God forgives her . . . I knew tonight would be the night I'd tell you the deepest, darkest secret of my life.

"I had an abortion. I was eighteen and away from home in college. I wasn't in love with the father of my baby, and I didn't want to take on the responsibility of having a child so young. I knew the shame of getting pregnant would hurt and disappoint my parents terribly. I didn't tell anyone, not even my best friend and roommate. I just made the appointment, took cash I had from a part-time job, and went to a clinic. It was over before I could think too much and change my mind. An abortion seemed to be the only solution for the situation I found myself in. I tried not to think about my baby. I told myself what people in the clinic said was true—it's just a mass of tissue; it will be over, and you can get on with your life.

"The guilt has plagued me for all these years. I've married and have two beautiful children. When I look at them, I wonder what their sibling would look like now if I had not made that fateful decision."

Susan continued to cry, releasing the trauma she had carried as she went on to live what seemed to be a perfect life. Her story is not so different from others I hear every time I tell my own story. Specific circumstances may change, but the emotions ignited by having an abortion are similar. Sometimes they rise to the surface soon after the procedure, but more often women manage to keep them submerged for years.

Susan told me that she felt a burden lifted as I talked because she could actually see me. She saw that I was a real woman who'd survived what she did to her own baby. I wasn't an abstract idea or a statistic.

"I've never thought about my unborn baby growing up to be like me or you or any individual person with a full life. I just couldn't think about that," she said through her tears.

Susan experienced freedom that night and decided to tell her loved ones about the baby who might have been in their family had she not had the abortion. She grabbed onto the glimmer of hope she'd heard about. If I could forgive my birth mother for trying to end my life twice, she could believe that her unborn baby could forgive her. And if God could forgive her, maybe her family could forgive her.

Many people's minds and hearts are already made up on issues surrounding abortion. At times the whole debate can take on an abstract or theoretical tone, as if these issues don't have any connection to our daily existence. But I'm not abstract or theoretical. I wasn't supposed to be alive, but here I am, living, breathing, and writing to you!

My lived experience amplifies the message I give whenever I speak: Every human life is precious. Every human life is a unique, valuable individual designed by God. Every human life is deserving of love, respect, and a chance at a full and vibrant existence.

When I say these statements, I come across as more than an advocate for an idea, more than a mouthpiece for a particular point of view. Looking at me, many people can see a personification of the millions of lives that could have been but instead never were.

PERSONAL ENCOUNTERS

A lot of people may think that I live a charmed life of travel and excitement without the everyday life of a wife and mother. But when I'm not traveling, I'm happy to enjoy my family while working on my ministry from home.

Sometimes I have two cleaning ladies help me get the house ready for my absence when I have speaking engagements. That way, David doesn't have to add cleaning to taking care of the kids and working his own job.

When they started coming, Nancy and Marianne and I would chat while we buzzed around the house. At different times, they each asked me what I did outside the home. We talked about it, and they gathered more information as they listened to me doing phone interviews or scheduling speaking engagements.

When I told Marianne what I did, her demeanor changed. She grew tense, her hands became balls of nervousness, tears welled up in her eyes, and I knew. I knew that look. It was the same look I saw in many of the women who approached me after I spoke at events. She had had an abortion.

She asked whether we could talk, so we moved over to the couch and sat. Marianne was crying by then and struggled to tell me her story. Regret weighed on her. She had been unable to get past what she had done.

I prayed with her, encouraged her, and told her about the hope she could have in God's love and forgiveness. Over the following months, Marianne and I talked while she cleaned, and I did more phone interviews and booked more speaking engagements. She absorbed so much of what she heard. Her heart began to heal as God redeemed her with his grace and mercy.

Marianne went on to participate in a post-abortion Bible study. She experienced a healing she had never thought was possible.

On another visit, Nancy said she wanted to tell me something. I stopped what I was doing, and we moved over to the same couch where Marianne and I had talked. Nancy told me that she had been raped years before and had decided to have the baby.

"I didn't think about getting an abortion," she said. "But even though I didn't have one, I think women should be able to get one if they make that choice."

We talked for a long time. Nancy didn't say she changed her mind about a woman's right to choose, but she listened attentively to me.

Not long ago, she called to let me know her thinking had changed. She told me that she had watched and listened over the last few years to the way I really cared about women . . . and their babies. She had recently talked with a woman who was considering an abortion, and Nancy wanted me to know that she had encouraged the woman not to go through with it.

"I changed my mind because of how loving you are, even to women who have had abortions," Nancy said.

I thanked her for the call. And as I hung up the phone, I thanked God for his grace in my life. I've made many mistakes and know forgiveness and grace firsthand. I want others to know that grace too.

I'm grateful for these opportunities and give all the praise to God for using me. I'm a shy person. No amount of effort on my part alone could have changed my shyness into outspokenness. God does that for me and uses me for his purposes.

God continues to move me through one open door after another as the number of people I reach grows. But that growth is his plan for me. I could never have imagined it.

Being called out of my comfort zone has been a thread throughout my life. When God put me on stages across the country to share my story, I knew he wouldn't stop there. I was being called to practice what I preached—to love women where they are, empower them to choose life, help make choosing life possible by walking alongside them, and so much more.

A FAMILY IN NEED

I didn't expect the phone call I received from a lady in town who had heard me speak, but that call made it evident that it was time for me to go beyond just telling my story onstage. It was time to bring women into my life who are looking for support when faced with the crisis of an unplanned pregnancy.

The lady on the phone that day said that she had just talked to a homeless woman, Grace, living in a tent on the side of the road. She was pregnant with no place to go. Would I help her? I went and talked to her and told her I would try to find a place for her to go and be cared for. But all the places I knew about were full. This woman was desperate. She had absolutely nothing and she was pregnant.

So Grace moved in with us and stayed for two months until Cody, her boyfriend, got a job and found a place for them to live. I took Grace to her doctor appointments and encouraged her to take care of herself. I cooked meals that always included nutrition she needed for the health of her baby. Grace became family, and as I got to know her more, I realized that she was just like so many other women in crisis. She was looking for someone to lift her up. I was fortunate to be able to do that and watch as she revealed who she was beyond the homelessness, the desperation, and the fear. On the other side of hopelessness, she found herself again—a beautiful and loving mother and friend.

Grace and Cody are married now, and they, along with Benjamin, the baby Grace was carrying six years ago, still visit us at least once a year. Benjamin has cystic fibrosis, so they come back to Austin for his annual checkup. When I asked Grace whether I could share her story, she said, "Of course! I wish everyone could know the real you, Claire. You helped me change my life!"

She is another example of God picking up a desperate person and helping that person find the path he has for him or her to follow. We are all broken and searching in one way or another. It's a story that is written all over my life and maybe yours too. Our brokenness brings us to our knees and causes us to search for goodness and truth, and once we grasp something worthwhile, we can choose to run after it. I have noticed something about the people God calls to greatness. He calls those who are broken and have a desperate need for him and hearts that are open to him working in their lives. That describes me at so many points of my life.

You may be reading this and asking yourself what you are called to do. I have to believe that he is going to use you if you let him, speak to you if you ask him to, and bring you to your knees only to lift you up and reveal his goodness and greatness. He will show himself as the best part of who you are as you serve and love others.

Every day, I remember that I spent a number of years as an apathetic, silent person when it came to abortion. Of course I still fail at times and don't always help in ways that I could. Missed opportunities to love others pass right by me as I fall short of what I could do.

I continue to work to love people well, but I struggle like everyone else with the demands of life. As I write this book, the COVID-19 pandemic has me housebound with three of my children. Homeschooling is a challenge. Loving well requires a lot of patience and includes a lot of saying "I'm sorry."

All any of us can do is make the best choices we can and hang on to the belief that God has us in the palm of his hand.

A FATHER'S RIGHTS

Originally I assumed that women were the main audience for my talks, so I largely targeted them with my messages. But in the last couple of years, I have changed my approach. I now direct specific messages to men every time I speak, because I see more and more of them as I look out over the audience. These men may need healing and forgiveness just as much as women do.

Plus, it's way past time for men to be brought into the abortion discussion. It takes two people to make a baby, and I believe both parents should be part of the entire process.

People may assume that women are the primary decision makers when it comes to abortion, but in many cases, men determine that abortion is the best way out of an unplanned pregnancy. They may pressure women to get an abortion and "take care of this problem."

Even when men aren't the decision makers, they may serve as enablers, whether by driving their girlfriends or daughters to the abortion clinic, helping pay for the procedure, or keeping the whole situation under wraps for the rest of their lives.

When I talk to men, I try to paint a picture for them. It's a scenario they may confront someday. Or maybe they already have. "Imagine for a moment that I am a pregnant teenager and you are my boyfriend," I say. "I'm scared, and I don't know what to do, just like my own birth mother didn't know what to do. My mom is pressuring me to get an abortion, and I ask you for help. Would you talk me through the life-and-death decision I'm about to make, or would you simply agree to drive me to the clinic and drop me off?"

I apologize to men for the fact that many women exclude them from decision-making about the babies they carry. Some women say, "This is my life. This is my body. This is my pregnancy. This is my decision. You don't have a role here. You need to stay out of this."

But I know from talking to many women that this is not exactly the way they all feel. Women who are all alone sometimes make decisions they wouldn't make if they knew the men in their lives would stand with them and walk with them through this difficult situation. Many of them long for the men to be strong amid crisis and confusion, help them, support them, and enable them to do the right thing, even if the right thing is the more difficult thing.

Legally speaking, fathers in the United States have no right to stop the abortion of a child they are responsible for. According to a BBC article entitled "The Men Who Feel Left Out of US Abortion Debate," some men want this to change. One man is even suing an Alabama abortion clinic after his girlfriend had an abortion against his wishes in 2017.[1]

Many of the men who come up and talk to me after my presentations have never given much thought to the issues surrounding abortion, while others have been haunted by thoughts about sons and daughters they could have had with past girlfriends.

Guilt sometimes strikes men after they get married, settle down, and start their own families. As they hold and play with their infant children, some fathers are surprised to feel overcome with a form of post-abortive grief. But they have no words to express it and no one to share it with.

It's never my intention to make men feel *more* guilt or grief. If they've been party to abortions, I want them to experience the same kind of forgiveness and healing that post-abortive women can know. But to realize forgiveness, we must sometimes take a brief journey through regret and repentance.

The worst time for making a life-and-death decision is when you're in the midst of a crisis. If men haven't been involved in these life-and-death discussions in the past, I hope they can be prepared in the future.

When I address men, I tell them, "It might be your own girlfriend who has an unplanned pregnancy. It might be a close male friend who seeks your advice about his girlfriend's pregnancy. It might be a coworker who confides in you. These urgent situations happen every day. What will you do when you face questions you never thought you would face?"

I go on to encourage them with a vision. "I hope that you men can be wise and godly servant-leaders in your relationships with women. I hope you can protect and preserve life in the decisions you make and the influence you exert on others. You have a voice. You have an important role to play. I hope you recognize this vision and fulfill it."

TALKING ABOUT FORGIVENESS

Forgiveness is another topic I include when speaking. I talk about forgiving Tonya for trying to abort me. It resonates with many women whether they have had an abortion or they need to forgive others for hurtful words or actions.

Many people respond like the woman who told me, "If you can forgive someone who did that to you, I should be able to forgive the people in my life for the things they do to me." The response of others is more troubled. "Now I wonder if the child I aborted will ever forgive me."

Again, it could seem that, in talking about forgiveness, I'm introducing guilt where there was none before. But it's more likely that some kind of regret or remorse was there before but was unacknowledged or unspoken.

Women and men who have been involved in abortion tell me that they hope the babies they aborted will one day forgive them. They believe, as I do, that the souls of unborn babies live on in heaven.

I believe those babies have forgiven their parents.

If we receive forgiveness for ourselves, we need to practice forgiveness of others. I'm not a preacher or Bible scholar, but consider the words of Jesus in Matthew 6:14: "For if you forgive other people when they sin against you, your heavenly Father will also forgive you."

Forgiveness is healing and rejuvenating. It has a way of opening up and airing out dank, dark areas of our lives that we've tried to keep closed and hidden for too long.

One night after I spoke about forgiving my birth mother, a man wept as he talked to me about the deep, dark secret he had kept hidden for so long. For years when he was a child, his parents—now dead—beat him, inflicting deep physical and emotional pain. They threatened that things would get worse if he informed on them, so he kept everything bottled up. Finally, well into his forties and tired of wrestling with demons from the past, the man told me he was going to work on forgiving his parents and freeing himself from their continuing control.

I'm grateful I can serve as a messenger of God's forgiveness to people who need it, and it's exciting to see that my own journey of forgiveness can inspire others to take that journey themselves.

One area where I have practiced forgiveness is also an area that produces complicated emotions for me. I feel a combination of grieving, wondering, and longing to know more about my twin who grew right alongside me inside our mother until the abortion took place. I don't experience survivor's guilt. That's not because my heart is hardened but because I simply trust God's perfect plan for me. Sure, I sometimes wonder why I was the one who survived. That's one of the many questions I want to ask God someday. Meanwhile, I know that he sees the bigger picture and I don't.

Did God have a special purpose and plan for me, even way back when I was in my mother's womb? Yes, and he has a special purpose and plan for you too.

I don't quote long passages of Scripture when I speak. I want people to know God's grace, not feel like they're getting hammered over the head with a Bible. But I often quote two passages that speak so clearly and powerfully about the life issues I address.

In Psalm 139, David praised God for his involvement in the miracle of human life: "You created my inmost being; you knit me together in my mother's womb" (verse 13). And the Old Testament prophet Jeremiah talked about how God knew him even before he was born: "Before I formed you in the womb I knew you" (Jeremiah 1:5).

Even though my emotions about this are complicated, I trust that God knows what he is doing. Trusting God was certainly a big part of my parents adopting me. They, like many couples, had hoped to have their own biological children. Because of that loss, many people may think of adoption as an inferior plan B. That's the way my mom and dad initially saw things as all their ministry friends were starting families. But after their experiences in adopting me and Rachel, they became full-fledged adoption advocates.

Adoption was plan B for my birth mother too. Of course, her plan A for me was abortion. I thank God that her plan A didn't work out. And I thank God that Warren and Barbara Culwell chose me and truly loved me and my sister, as they always assured us, more than anyone has ever loved their children.

After talking with many adoptees, I realize that, sadly, not all adopted children find themselves in loving, caring homes. Rachel and I grew up never doubting our parents' love for us or their joy that we were the children who came into their lives. But other adoptees aren't always so fortunate. They don't always receive as much love as we did. They don't always get good explanations about their origins. Some grow up with questions about their identity and aren't so sure about themselves. Some never get over their feelings that their biological parents rejected or abandoned them.

I try to encourage adoptees to be thankful. Thankful for the lives they've lived. Thankful for the people who have cared for them—even if their experiences weren't as wonderful as mine. I encourage them to be grateful for their parents—the ways they loved well and the many things they did right. And I nudge adoptees to forgive their parents for the things they did that didn't turn out so well.

I also encourage adoptees to focus *less* on the imperfections of their earthly adoptive parents and *more* on the perfection of their heavenly Father. As Psalm 139 says, it was God who knit us together and knew us in our mothers' wombs. God gave us the gift of life. I want everyone to be thankful for this good gift, even if the opening chapters of our life stories weren't picture perfect.

Whenever I get the chance, I plead with everyone who hears me to make adoption a viable option for frightened couples who believe the best solution to an unplanned pregnancy is a quick abortion. Adoption is a good thing and can be a wonderful thing, as many of the five million American adoptees—and millions more around the world—already know.[2]

ADOPTION OPTIONS

Over the years, I've had the opportunity to meet and talk with many devoted pastors, priests, and lay leaders who are committed to making their churches pro-life congregations. But as I've talked with some of these men and women, I've discovered a troubling reality.

Many pro-life Christians assume that it's not God-loving, Bible-reading Christian women who are having abortions but *those other women* who are killing their babies. While it's true that many women who have abortions have no deep, abiding faith in Christ, many of these women are committed Christians who pray, read the Bible, and regularly attend church.

The problem of abortion isn't just "them," the people outside our churches' walls. The problem is also us. "Many women with unplanned pregnancies go silently from the church pew to the abortion clinic, convinced the church would gossip rather than help," according to a 2015 study commissioned by Care Net, a pro-life ministry founded in 1975 and inspired by Christian scholar Francis Schaeffer and former US surgeon general C. Everett Koop.[3]

"More than four in ten women who have had an abortion were churchgoers when they ended a pregnancy," according to the study, which was conducted by LifeWay Research. "But only 7 percent of women discussed their abortion decision with anyone at church."[4] The survey of 1,038 women who have had abortions revealed these startling statistics:

- Sixty-five percent say "church members judge single women who are pregnant."
- Fifty-four percent think "churches oversimplify decisions about pregnancy options."
- Forty-one percent believe "churches are prepared to help women with their decisions about unwanted pregnancies."
- Only thirty-eight percent consider church "a safe place

to talk about pregnancy options" including parenting, abortion, and adoption.

- Women say they expected or experienced judgment (33 percent) or condemnation (26 percent) from a church far more than caring (16 percent) or helpfulness (14 percent).[5]

This study reveals a sad reality about the way many believers treat women who are confronting life-and-death decisions. Instead of telling women who are facing unplanned pregnancies that God's family is there to help them and their babies, churches often send messages that these women have blown it, committed an unpardonable sin, and forsaken their faith. The Guttmacher Institute, an organization that supports abortion, found similar statistics in its own 2014 study:

> The majority of abortion patients indicated a religious affiliation: Seventeen percent identified as mainline Protestant, 13% as evangelical Protestant and 24% as Roman Catholic, while 8% identified with some other religion. Thirty-eight percent of patients did not identify with any religion.[6]

These studies confirm what I see in too many churches today. Whether they mean to or not, many strong, pro-life churches proclaim a harsh message that abortion is murder and that women who have had abortions have put themselves beyond the reach of God's love and grace.

Many churches teach about the sin of premarital sex or married infidelity. If a pregnancy occurs in these situations, the church either is silent or shames the woman for the act that resulted in her pregnancy. Most teaching to young people focuses on the admonition not to have sex but is silent on why they shouldn't or how the church should respond if they do have sex and a pregnancy results.

I don't speak to kids (or adults) about sex. What I do talk about is the silence of the church on behalf of the unmarried pregnant girl or woman in their midst. Of course, repentance is needed when any sin is committed, but I believe the first issue to talk about is the support and care the girl or woman should be able to expect from the Christian community she is part of.

Jesus went to the cross and died for our—and her—sins. He didn't wait until the whole world repented to pay the price for our sins. Whether or not the girl or woman displays deep repentance, the life inside her exists.

Imagine how helpful it would be if girls or women in this difficult situation turned first to the church for guidance and support. What if churches embraced these women and offered to help them carry their babies to birth and then supported them as they placed their babies for adoption or raised them? Wouldn't that be the Christlike thing to do?

I believe that the church needs to be as concerned about the unborn babies they could save as they are about rebuking the sin that caused the pregnancies. God can bring girls and women into close relationships with Christ and redeem the mistakes they have made. He can bring them into newness of life as they learn, grow, and experience the gracious love he offers.

A VISION FOR CHURCHES

The book of Proverbs says, "Where there is no vision, the people perish" (29:18, KJV). If I were to write down my vision for churches, these items would be at the top of my list.

I have a vision of churches full of people who celebrate life, no matter the origin of each life. I have a vision of churches full of people who are caring and gracious enough to reach out in love and support when women and men struggle with unplanned pregnancies. I have a vision of churches full of pro-life advocates who will commit themselves to walking alongside these struggling men and women to help them embrace life, whether that be through parenting or through the gift of adoption.

I have spoken in many churches that are working to make this dream a reality. The programs aren't always perfect, but they're in place and they're helping women and men in desperate need. Unfortunately, there are still too many churches that haven't done much to translate their pro-life rhetoric into programs that help people in need.

But that's changing.

Let me introduce you to some of the churches and other organizations that are making a difference for people who wrestle with unplanned pregnancies.

Sanctuary of Hope

Sanctuary of Hope, a ministry of Cornerstone Church in San Antonio, Texas, does many of the things I dream more churches would do. It provides care and nurture to single expectant mothers and their children, including housing and counseling.

John Hagee, Cornerstone Church's founding pastor, worked at an orphanage when he was a teenager more than half a century ago, and ever since, he had dreamed of creating a ministry that would serve children who had been rejected and had no family. Finally, in the last few years, Sanctuary of Hope was born to fulfill this vision:

What if we could offer a viable alternative that gives young mothers, and their precious unborn children, the option of LIFE, and the possibility of a productive future?

We don't believe that abortion should ever be the answer, but it is not enough to simply believe—we must continue to take a moral and Biblical stand against this practice and provide an alternative for these young mothers who at times feel they have no other option. With your help, we will give them, and their unborn children, a future and a hope.[7]

The Austin Stone Community Church

For many years, I attended the Austin Stone Community Church, a multicampus megachurch in Austin. The church has a ministry called For the City that reaches out to people in the community who have needs.

One of the ministries they've launched is designed to love and care for people facing unplanned pregnancies. They also want to minister to post-abortive men and women. I helped Austin Stone create a video they use as a conversation starter around these issues.

Young Life's YoungLives

Young Life, the youth ministry founded in 1941, now works with young people in more than one hundred countries. In the 1990s, "Young Life answered God's call to run headfirst into the chaos of teenage motherhood with the hope of Jesus . . . and YoungLives was born."

The vision is "to reach teen moms by entering their world,

modeling the unconditional love of Christ, and encouraging them to become the women and mothers God created them to be."

The program matches young moms with "older experienced moms who are committed to providing support and friendship as well as the opportunity to consider the possibility of a relationship with Jesus Christ."[8]

Embrace Grace

The vision of Embrace Grace, listed on their website, is clear: "For every girl with an unplanned pregnancy to have a church to go to for spiritual, emotional and physical support."

They're making that vision real in a way that is simple and direct: "We help women with unplanned pregnancies find a place of belonging within the church through support groups."

Embrace Grace has some seven hundred active support groups, and they have helped more than six thousand women work through the challenges of unplanned pregnancies. As their website says, "The church has a powerful opportunity to be a catalyst of change in a woman's life as well as broaden their community outreach to help moms be brave."[9]

You don't need a famous megachurch, celebrity pastor, or big parachurch organization in order to reach out to people dealing with unplanned pregnancies. Even small churches can communicate to men and women that they have a safe place, a loving Christian community that will have their backs when they face the unexpected.

PLANS FOR GOOD

The main message of my life story is a simple one: God can turn difficult things into beautiful things. Think about it. I had a near-death experience before I was even born. That's not a good way to start things out. But thirty some years later, I couldn't be happier or more grateful for the life I've lived, the lives I have given birth to and parented, the lives I have touched through my speaking ministry.

My birth mother tried to abort me, but God had a better plan for me. He has a better plan for you too. The prophet Jeremiah talked about this:

> "I know the plans I have for you," declares the LORD, "plans
> to prosper you and not to harm you, plans to give you hope
> and a future." (Jeremiah 29:11)

God uses things that were meant for evil and turns them into things that are beautiful and fruitful, like he did with me. Bad things have been transformed into beautiful things in my life. My journey has included plenty of pain and bumps in the road, but God took someone destined for death and turned me into an advocate for life. He took something bad and made it into something very good. Now that I can see the bigger picture, I truly appreciate that I survived, grew up, and now have my own family.

It's possible you have something in your life that's painful and doesn't make any sense at this moment. You, too, can trust in the God that sees the bigger picture and experience the transformation that takes place when the heart moves from fear to trust.

One woman who knew how to do this was Mary, the mother of Jesus. She faced a seemingly bad situation. She was a teenager who was pregnant out of wedlock and living in a very traditional religious culture. The society all around her dismissed her and judged her. It's amazing to me that her husband-to-be, Joseph, stuck around.

It must have been a troubling time for Mary, but she trusted God, put her fate in his hands, and gave birth to the baby boy who would save the world. At the time, she couldn't see the bigger picture, but we can all see it now.

12.

EXPERIENCING GOD'S GRACE AND REDEMPTION

. . .

*D*URING MY SPEAKING ENGAGEMENTS BEFORE MY pregnancy, I didn't comment on specific legislation. I was a storyteller, and I was happy to share my own story as a powerful way to advocate for unborn babies.

But the more I was exposed to the various laws being passed or not passed, I felt that my calling from God was being enlarged. How abortion is presented to the public touches the lives of all women making decisions to save their unborn babies or to have abortions, and that presentation ultimately impacts legislation. I could hear God's whisper in my spirit to walk boldly through the next door he was opening for me.

I have to admit that I'm glad I didn't know in college how God's plan for my life would unfold. If I had seen myself on platforms that continued to grow larger, I might have headed to nursing school and refused to keep listening to God's call. Nursing is a noble and needed profession. And I'm grateful for those who choose that life path. But if I had stayed with that choice, I would have been running away from what God had for me because of fear.

One of the groups that decided to keep me as a speaker during my pregnancy was a Canadian organization sponsoring an educational conference for two thousand to three thousand people.

I was about twenty-five weeks pregnant and sporting a big baby bump, and I stood on a stage and shared my story of surviving abortion, loving adoption, and becoming part of the pro-life movement. I felt my baby girl—who had been busily wriggling around during the whole talk—deliver an especially strong kick to my belly. That kick inspired me to comment on Canada's permissive abortion laws.

"You know," I told the group, "here in Canada abortion is completely legal, even at my advanced stage of pregnancy. If I decided that the life growing inside me was inconvenient or I simply didn't want her any longer, I could go to a clinic in Canada right now and have an abortion for any reason."

I thought back to my latest sonogram. My baby's growth was right on track, and everything was developing rapidly: her fingers, her toes, the tiny features of her face.

"It wouldn't make any difference at the clinic that she is an active, healthy baby, apparently with a very strong foot."

My emphasis had always been on persuasion, not legislation. I wanted to change hearts and minds, not laws. But the fact that I was carrying an extremely active life that was not protected by Canadian law bothered me, and I let them know it. It turned out it would not be the last time I commented on abortion laws.

A few months after Sadie June was born, I got a call from Joe Pojman from the Texas Alliance for Life. I knew Joe from speak-

ing at some TAL functions. Now he said he had a favor he wanted
to ask me.

"Claire, there's a pro-life legislation called House Bill 2 that
I've been lobbying in the Texas legislature," he said. "The bill
passed the house and will be introduced on the senate floor in a few
days.

"Could you come and testify in behalf of the bill on the senate
floor? I'm going to testify, and so is Abby. We believe your unique
perspective as a survivor of abortion could be powerful. What do
you think, Claire?"

"I'd be honored, Joe," I told him without studying the legislation or realizing what kind of circus I was about to enter.

I had zero experience in legislation. I saw my testimony at the
statehouse as an opportunity to share my story with an audience
that had never heard it before, offering them a message of hope and
healing.

Joe explained that I would have three minutes to talk, and if I
went over my time by a second, a buzzer would sound and I would
be gaveled and told to sit down. During my testimony, I would
stand at a podium facing about a dozen Texas legislators, while,
behind me, members of the public and the news media would fill
the rest of the chamber.

I pared down my normal talk to the bare minimum, writing out
the entire speech instead of relying on my trusty bullet items. I
practiced it again and again to make sure I would not exceed my
time, even if I had trouble catching my breath because of my nervousness.

House Bill 2 had become Senate Bill 5 by the time I testified.
The legislation's provisions would ban abortions twenty weeks
after conception and require doctors practicing abortions to have
admitting privileges at a nearby hospital. The bill's language was

similar to legislation that would be proposed in other states in the years to come.

Pro-lifers loved the bill, but the pro-choice crowd hated it and feared it would restrict women's access to abortion across the state. They brought a crowd of protesters to the capitol, filling the chamber and a number of nearby overflow rooms.

In a previous chapter I've expressed my frustration with angry *pro-life* activists who yell and scream at pregnant women to get their point across. On the morning I showed up at the statehouse, I had my first opportunity to experience angry *pro-choice* activists who yelled and screamed at their pro-life opponents, including me. They carried signs with words too graphic to repeat. I was shocked and I felt threatened. As I walked through the crowd, it struck me how people on both sides of this issue can express their passions in ways too hurtful to produce helpful results. It's a sad reality.

Later, inside the legislative chamber, pro-choice advocates disrupted the proceedings. Dozens were arrested. What had I gotten myself into? I felt like a newbie in the pro-life movement, and suddenly it seemed like I would be confronting pro-choice veterans who had honed their arguments and tested their tactics. I was way out of my comfort zone.

When my name was called, I stood and unsteadily walked to the podium. Between big gulps of air, I carefully read the speech I had written out and practiced, keeping my eye on the clock to make sure I didn't exceed my allotted time. I finished my final thought as the buzzer rang, and I took my seat while the next person testifying rose and went toward the podium.

I had been asked to speak and had survived the ordeal. Now everything was in the hands of the legislature. But things were about to get even crazier. The next day a pro-choice lawmaker named Wendy Davis decided she would filibuster the bill. If you've ever seen the classic Hollywood movie *Mr. Smith Goes to Washington,* filibustering is what actor James Stewart's character engaged in, talking himself ragged over a period of hours in order to delay a vote on a crucial bill.

Senator Davis stood up to speak on the last day of the June legislative session, and her goal was to speak until midnight. If she did so, the session would end without allowing an opportunity for a vote on Senate Bill 5.

She started talking and didn't stop, even though one legislator claimed she had changed topics, which would've technically ended her filibuster. But she persisted, speaking until after midnight. I attended the session that day but lasted only until 7:00 p.m. I had Sadie June with me, so there was no way I would have stayed until midnight. I later heard that when she stopped talking, pro-choice activists cheered. Senate Bill 5 was dead. Or so they thought.

But then Governor Rick Perry responded, calling a special session of the legislature to vote on the bill, which later passed. This was my first chance to see the legislative process up close, and while it was not always pretty, democratic processes prevailed, and the bill passed, leading to a drastic decrease in the number of Texas abortion clinics.

I don't know whether my testimony helped these efforts, but I was glad to add my voice to the others defending life. Soon I would be invited to testify in other states, and my schedule would get busier.

Following the surprising election of Donald Trump as president of the United States in 2016, dozens of states would seek to enact new abortion restrictions in 2017, 2018, and 2019.

Trump had previously been pro-choice, but his position

changed several years before he was voted into office.[1] His vice president, Mike Pence; his secretary of housing and urban development, Ben Carson; and other members of his administration had been strongly pro-life for many years.

After Trump's election and after he nominated a fifth conservative justice to the Supreme Court, many states seized the moment and introduced new legislation. More than half a dozen of these states asked me to come testify in behalf of their legislation.

As an abortion survivor, many legislators saw me as a positive public face of the pro-life movement, as well as a warning about the lives that abortion takes. I traveled from state to state, and in the process, the adjective *activist* was added to my profile. By 2019, I had lent my voice to several pro-life bills around the country.

- Texas. I spoke at a press conference and testified before senate and house committees. Representative Jeff Leach acknowledged me on the house floor, and Governor Greg Abbott featured me in an ad for his reelection campaign, which included strong opposition to abortion and strong support for adoption.
- Kentucky. I testified before senate and house committees. Senator Matt Castlen acknowledged me on the senate floor, and I had a meet-and-greet session with Governor Matt Bevin. His office released a video of our time together to express his support for pro-life legislation.
- Massachusetts, North Carolina, and Wisconsin. In capitols of these states, I spoke at press conferences for pro-life bills.
- I provided written testimony that was used to support pro-life laws in numerous other states.

- And in our nation's capital, I was acknowledged on the US House and Senate floors by legislators numerous times and spoke on the same stage as President Trump at the Values Voter Summit in October 2019.

In a very real sense, it was legislation restricting abortion that saved me from a second attempted abortion and gave me my life. Tonya was already five months pregnant with me when she went to get the abortion that I survived.

But when Tonya's mother ordered her to get another abortion to finally end my life, it was too late. Legislation preventing third-trimester abortions saved my life. Without that law, I would have been an abortee, not an adoptee. I would have been dead, not alive.

Still, I believe my calling within the larger pro-life movement is *persuasion, not legislation,* because laws alone can never end abortion in America or anywhere else.

My personal mission has always focused on encouraging people to choose life and supporting them for doing so, not relying on legislation that restricts people's options. But different people are called to bring different skills to pro-life issues, and all of us need to work together to reduce and eliminate abortion in America.

We need to work on all fronts: enacting legislation, changing the stigma surrounding adoption, supporting families choosing life, and filling the gaps in women's health care as we shut down abortion clinics. Changing hearts and minds on abortion is still the key, but many methods must work in coordination.

Whenever someone asks what I think pro-lifers should be doing in their fight against abortion, I always respond with four things:

1. *Speak the truth:* No matter how you are communicating your message—with words, actions, or attitudes—show respect for your listeners. You may not agree with their stand on this issue, but their hearts and minds will never change if they feel disrespected. Pray before opening your mouth or writing a word.

2. *Offer help instead of insults:* Women going into abortion clinics are hoping for an answer to a difficult situation. They are looking for a way out. They are much more likely to respond to kind offers of help than to angry signs or cruel slogans.

3. *Offer to help them through the process of saving their babies' lives:* They may well have a rough road ahead and may consider a choice other than abortion if they know they will have help all the way through.

4. *Encourage them:* These women probably don't feel strong or courageous. Encourage them with words that communicate a positive outcome for them.

BIG CROWD IN
THE BIG APPLE

An invitation to speak in 2019 offered an opportunity to address the largest crowd I'd ever faced. It was May 4, 2019, and a gathering of close to twenty thousand people were jammed into New York City's Times Square for Alive from New York, the largest pro-life event ever held there.

It was a huge crowd in a huge city, and there was little old me, the still-shy introvert, right in the middle of them all. I couldn't believe I was there. I felt grateful, excited, overwhelmed, nervous, and fully in the moment. I would be speaking along with famous leaders who were loved by the crowd:

- Alveda King, the civil rights activist who is a niece of Dr. Martin Luther King Jr.
- Cardinal Timothy Dolan, the archbishop of New York and an outspoken pro-lifer
- Jeanne Mancini, president of March for Life
- Marjorie Dannenfelser, president of Susan B. Anthony List
- Carter Conlon, senior pastor of Times Square Church
- Jim Daly, president of Focus on the Family, which organized the whole event

Alive from New York had been planned as a way to celebrate the sanctity of human life and encourage women facing unplanned pregnancies to choose life—either by becoming a mother or by placing the child for adoption—rather than choosing death by abortion.

I was one of three abortion survivors who would tell their stories. This was the first time in history that three survivors would appear on the same stage. I had already met the other two survivors the previous February when we appeared together on Fox News, which regularly covers the pro-life movement.

There was Melissa Ohden, who survived an abortion in 1977 and, like me, has become a pro-life speaker and activist. She told her story in the book *You Carried Me: A Daughter's Memoir*.[2] As the founder of the Abortion Survivors Network, she has been in contact with more than two hundred abortion survivors.

Also, there was Josiah Presley. Josiah miraculously survived a curettage abortion, which involves ripping a baby apart inside the mother's womb and bringing the baby out piece by piece. He now works as a youth pastor at a church in Mesquite, Texas.

The air was filled with excitement as one of the event organizers escorted Melissa, Josiah, and me from the hotel to a restaurant near the stage that was serving as the green room. We chatted nervously for about thirty minutes before being taken backstage for media interviews.

The stage was set up in the street facing Times Square. Crowds filled the street as far as we could see right up to the giant video screen that would broadcast this event.

As I got ready to go on, pictures of me as an infant and little girl flashed across the screen that formed the backdrop of the stage. It felt surreal to be seeing those images just before taking the platform. I had been given three minutes to speak.

I walked up on the stage and was handed the mic. I silently prayed, *God, please don't let me forget what I want to say,* even though I held a card with six bullet points to remind me. I looked out at the sea of eager faces and wondered whether they could hear my heart beating.

I said that my birth mother had told me that she would never have had an abortion if someone had stood up for her. I also said that Melissa, Josiah, and I needed to be the last of the people who would carry the title of "abortion survivor." We had all been hurt by the abortions our birth mothers had, but we were alive today to stand up for an end to abortion.

I finished, and the crowd erupted in applause!

Now I could relax and reflect on the importance of this event. Along with encouraging women to choose life for their babies, the event was intended to challenge a new abortion law in New York State. The Reproductive Health Act had been signed into law the previous January on the forty-sixth anniversary of the famous

Roe v. Wade Supreme Court ruling that permitted abortion across the United States.

Prior to the passage of the Reproductive Health Act, New York law banned third-trimester abortions except when the mother's life was at risk. Now, with the passing of the act, abortion could be performed at any time.

Focus on the Family, which has been a pioneering pro-family and pro-life ministry for decades, relies on the persuasive power of ultrasound images that show unborn babies in their mothers' wombs. Focus sponsors a program that helps provide ultrasound machines to pregnancy centers so that women considering abortions may reconsider after seeing life growing inside them.

After my talk, the concluding event was not another speaker or musical performance but a live 4D ultrasound image of a baby. The goal had been to broadcast the live 4D image on some of the gigantic digital screens that face Times Square and typically feature advertising images. But there was a last-moment hitch. Three companies who owned the digital screens declined to lease space on their screens for the ultrasound projection.

"In many ways, this blockade only confirms what we've long known," wrote Jim Daly on his blog. "There are many people who don't want the world to see these images of pre-born life, because the abortion industry is predicated on a lie—namely that a baby is just a blob of tissue inside the womb. It's not. It's a baby."[3]

The giant screens may not have been available, but the screen on the stage was. The announcer told the crowd that the moment they had been waiting for was about to happen: an ultrasound of a pregnant woman's baby was being taken backstage in a mobile ultrasound unit and would be projected live any minute! The image appeared to the enthusiastic cheers of the crowd.

Just when the crowd thought the excitement was over, the announcer told them that the next speaker was the woman whose ultrasound they had just seen. That's when Abby Johnson walked out from behind the screen and the whole place went crazy. The people there were so excited to have shared those ultrasound moments with her.

"We will see a day when abortion in this country is unthinkable!" Abby said to the cheering crowd. Media coverage of the event included the headline "ALIVE from New York: The Day Abortion Died."[4]

Most people went home after Alive from New York was over, but not Abby and me. We spent one more night in New York so we would be ready for our early-morning appointment the next day: a live appearance on Fox News at 6:00 a.m.

The cable channel had covered Alive from New York and wanted to do some follow-up segments featuring the two speakers who had concluded the event.

I got up at 4:00 a.m. to shower and get dressed in time to be picked up by a limo just after 5:00 a.m. After a short drive, we checked into the Fox studios at 5:20. We were taken to the makeup room, where people worked to make us ready for the bright lights and cameras and offered us coffee and croissants. Then we were rushed toward the studio. We walked down a big hall while technicians wired us with microphones and a producer announced the countdown.

Forty seconds.

Thirty seconds.

Twenty seconds.

We were finally seated in the studio.

Ten seconds.

By the time the cameras went live, I was struggling to catch my breath. But I had little time to breathe deeply, because I needed to speak quickly during each of the three segments that featured us. The longest segment was eight minutes, and the two others lasted about three to four minutes.

It's a lot of work for a brief amount of time, but in some ways, appearing on TV is easier than speaking before large groups. You can reach an audience of millions without having to deal with the worst parts of stage fright. The hardest thing for me is compressing my complicated life story into powerful sound bites that make for good TV.

By the time my breathing calmed down, our appearances were over. I let out a big sigh. It had been a chaotic two days. I was ready to return to my normal life outside the glare of the spotlight.

As we were leaving the studio, Abby stopped and turned to me. She smiled her big, happy smile, and I smiled too. Here we were . . . a former abortion clinic director and a survivor of an abortion that took the life of my twin. We were standing in a TV studio after appearing together before millions of people to advocate for the lives of unborn babies.

Only God could have brought us together and created the friendship we now have as he uses both our stories for the same cause.

After so much excitement, I wanted to get back to my home and family. I thought about the people who ask me how I manage speaking while juggling my life with my husband and four children. They want to know what an average day looks like when I'm home. I love to answer those questions because they show how human I am. I'm not just a person traveling around, talking from a platform. I'm so grateful that I get to do that, but my real life is at home.

Our weekday routine is probably similar to many families'.

David pops out of bed by 6:00 a.m., makes coffee (and graciously brings me a cup), gets dressed, and heads out to work by 6:30 so he can open the Austin location of Core Supply.

Once my coffee kicks in, I jump into my morning routine of getting up and getting the kids ready for school. I drop off eleven-year-old Lita and eight-year-old Sadie June at elementary school and get eighteen-year-old Dylan and thirteen-year-old Elijah (we call him Eli) off to their buses.

When I get home from my morning rounds, it's time for cleanup and catch-up. I clean up around the house, prepare dinner, and take care of other domestic duties while also catching up on activities related to my speaking ministry.

On a typical day, I may record a brief video that the groups hosting me can use to promote their events, respond to a few emails from people who reached out to me at a previous speaking engagement, and post something on my social media accounts for the people who follow me.

Then, before I know it, it's time for the afternoon routine of picking up kids, taking them to their afternoon activities (soccer for the girls, band practice for Eli), and running errands.

I'm the kind of mom who likes to be involved in my children's education, so I'm part of the parent-teacher organization at my kids' schools, volunteering in various ways, serving teachers when I can, and helping plan special events.

Sometime between 4:30 and 5:00, David gets home from work and dives right into playing with and talking to the kids.

We believe it's important for all six of us to have dinner together every night, at least when possible. We pray together, dig into the food, and talk about our days.

Then we typically gather in the family room to watch television. We love shows like *America's Got Talent* and *American Idol,* a show I've been watching since high school. I love to hear people's stories and watch as their dreams come true.

We pray with the kids before they go to bed; then it's time for David and me to sit and talk or watch something on TV if we have the energy to stay awake. When I don't have much energy, I go to bed when the kids do.

We try to have weekly date nights, with David's parents keeping an eye on the kids, but that doesn't always work out with our schedules.

Weekends are different. It seems like I live at soccer fields most Saturdays, cheering on the girls as they play. On Sundays, we go to Hill Country Bible Church. We try to get to my parents' house for a Sunday meal every other week or so.

Of course, everything changes when I'm out of town speaking. David must step in and take over my roles. Thankfully, his job gives him the flexibility to take care of the kids when I'm gone. What a relief!

Only rarely is David able to travel with me, and even when he does, he doesn't announce himself. Like me, he's an introvert, and he's more than content to leave the spotlight to me.

A POWERFUL STORY

When Tonya and I reconnected the second time, a lot of healing had happened for both of us. Thankfully, we now enjoy an ongoing relationship.

That relationship led us to become the faces of Sanctuary of Hope.

At one point, the organization decided to produce a video about our story. First the video team came to film my parents and me, and then they wanted to film Tonya at her home. I flew out to Tonya's house to support her while she filmed her segment. Once I arrived, I got reacquainted with the cameraman, Gary, who had filmed my parents' segment. He greeted Tonya, and it was obvious that she was very nervous. Gary was patient and gently talked Tonya through her story.

As Tonya responded to Gary's questions, I realized it was the first time I had heard her express her feelings to someone else. Her emotions flowed out of her.

I heard her again say, "Being pregnant at thirteen is horrible. You feel humiliated . . . You're trapped . . . My mother said, 'You're gonna do this, and we're gonna shut up about it, and no one's gonna know, and you're gonna go back to school, and you're gonna act like things are normal.' "

She'd trusted her mother. She didn't have anyone else to trust. She didn't have anyone else to give her guidance. Tonya said that if she had known about a place like Sanctuary of Hope, she would have gone there. She looks at what they provide and knows that their care of single pregnant women saves so many lives.

Through all the filming, Gary set the tone. His kindness and gentle manner communicated to Tonya that she was safe. He was safe. He would portray her as her true self. He acknowledged how terribly hard it must have been for Tonya and asked her heartfelt questions.

After he left, we were walking around her property. She looked at me and said, "For the first time, I finally feel free. It hurts, but I feel like a huge weight was lifted off my shoulders. The cameraman really touched me. I felt seen and heard and cared for."

Gary is still in our lives. We stay in touch, and he has said on more than one occasion, "Yours is the most powerful story I've ever heard."

He played a huge part in Tonya's story that day. His gentle manner freed her, and she was transformed because of him. What could have been a traumatic experience became a blessing.

BEING ON SET

A few months later, the movie *Unplanned* was going to be filming in Stillwater, Oklahoma. They were going to be shooting a part of Abby's story in a reconstruction of an abortion clinic. Abby invited me to visit the set, and I asked Tonya whether she wanted to join me.

Stillwater is so close to Tonya's home that it gave me a chance to see her again. And more importantly, it is the town where Tonya had the abortion I survived.

Tonya and I walked slowly into the abortion clinic set. I watched her expression change as we got to the room set up to film the abortion procedure. She stood still and stared around the room. Tears spilled out of her eyes.

"I lay on a table just like this one," she said as she touched the edge of the cold, hard surface.

An almost-inaudible gasp came out of her mouth as she looked at a machine next to the table. "I watched my baby suctioned out of my body by a machine just like this one."

I moved close to Tonya and put my arm around her as she relived all those emotions she had experienced as a thirteen-year-old girl. I can't imagine how helpless and scared she must have felt.

Later, we had dinner with Abby and some of her closest friends and pro-life associates. She talked about how God had used her brokenness and sin to bring healing to so many. She went on to say how hard it had been for her to forgive herself.

I thought back to our time at the Holocaust Memorial Museum in DC, where I had found Abby crumpled on the floor in tears over what she had done. I had seen one of those moments when her guilt overwhelmed her. Now she stood in front of a small group of close friends and spoke with the confidence of someone who had been touched by God's forgiving hand. His love and grace had redeemed her. She was whole.

Tonya leaned over and whispered to me, "If Abby can forgive herself for what she's done, maybe I can believe that God forgives me."

I'd witnessed another milestone moment in Tonya's life when God brought her closer to himself.

LOVE BROUGHT US TOGETHER

In November 2019, I was asked to speak at a gala outside Nashville for a pro-life group called Voice of Choice. Then, two days before the event, organizers called me with a surprise.

"Hey, Claire, we just wanted to let you know that we are flying Tonya in to see you speak, and we would like to film the two of you together."

Perhaps they were expecting me to jump for joy, but Tonya had never heard me speak before, and having this sprung on me upset me.

"You did what?" I asked.

Before they could answer, I said, "No, it isn't best for her to come be on the stage."

I knew how threatening it could feel to be in front of a live group. I didn't want her to revisit her guilt in what could turn out to be an unsafe place. Sometimes an audience can convey hurtful feelings without saying a word. But I recognized that I wasn't thinking just about Tonya. Since she hadn't heard me speak in person yet, I felt I might be trying to protect myself as well.

I got off the phone and dissolved into a puddle of tears. It was 6:00 a.m., and I'd have to get the kids up soon for school. I went into the closet and called my parents. They still are my human anchors when I feel frantic. I told them what was happening and that I wasn't ready to look Tonya in the eye while I spoke in front of a group. I felt taken advantage of and vulnerable. My emotions got the best of me.

Mom and Dad assured me that I had every right to feel that way and could just call the Nashville group back and tell them I wasn't okay with her being at this event.

"But," my mom said, "don't call right away. Sit on it awhile, and see if this could be good in any way. Maybe this is a piece of the puzzle of your life that God is using. Could it be that God is getting you even more out of your comfort zone, where he uses you best?"

I got off the phone and came out of the closet, scolding myself for such silly behavior. There was no time to do anything but wait to make a decision as I scurried around, getting the children up and off to school.

But I didn't have to sit on it for long. As soon as my mom told me to think about how this might be another way God wanted more courage from me, I knew that I would agree to have Tonya come.

I did let the Nashville group know that she would be fine with them filming her. She had cleared that hurdle and should be okay with doing it again. She did agree, and the filming happened before the gala. As I understood the plan, they would play the film before

I spoke, Tonya would be in the audience, and I would speak and then bring her up on the stage and introduce her.

That's not what happened.

The day of the event, Tonya and I were arriving in Nashville at the same time. My flight landed a few minutes before hers, so I walked over to her gate. The doors were just opening into the terminal as I got there. Tonya came through those doors with the biggest grin on her face. She caught my eye and waved, and I knew—she was healed. She was ready for the next part of our journey.

That night, we went into the ballroom where I would be speaking. As we approached the stage, I saw the screen set up for Tonya's video, and slightly off to the side, two chairs were placed next to each other. Tonya and I would be on the stage together. We were told that she would sit in the first row while I spoke and then sit next to me while her video was played.

I was more nervous than I'd been at Alive from New York. When it was time for me to speak, I went to the microphone and looked out across the glittering ballroom. Well-dressed men and women enjoying a fundraising dinner turned their attention to me, and I turned to Tonya.

I looked into her eyes and was filled with love for her. I wanted to honor her. I wanted to honor God and the story he was writing in both our lives.

After I spoke, Tonya was brought up to sit next to me onstage while they played the video of her telling her part of our story. She cried as she watched herself tell of her experience. I cried as I watched her relive every word and emotion. The video ended, and I walked back to the microphone.

"I would now like to introduce you to my birth mother. You

will not only see the face of a woman who has experienced abortion and its aftermath, but you will see a beautiful woman who has healed by the grace and redemption of God. May I introduce my birth mother, Tonya Glasby."

The audience erupted in applause. Tonya grabbed my hand and held both our hands high in the air. We stood there, arms uplifted, claiming the victory of lives transformed. We were survivors, and by Christ alone, our story had been redeemed!

That was our breakthrough moment, our victory celebration. Death had tried to drive us apart, but love brought us together.

EPILOGUE

Connecting the Dots

. . .

*J*ANUARY IS TYPICALLY MY BUSIEST MONTH OF THE YEAR. That's when March for Life holds its big rally in Washington, DC, and many smaller rallies and other events happen in cities across the country. The timing of these events commemorates the most important date in pro-life history: the Supreme Court's January 22, 1973, ruling in *Roe v. Wade* that legalized abortion across America. In January 2020, I spoke at the national March for Life gathering in DC as well as local gatherings in Oklahoma and Texas.

As I traveled to and from these events over the course of a few days, I marveled anew at how God had composed a beautiful story for my life, a story that connected the different episodes of my life: my near death by abortion, my surprising birth, my amazing adoption experience, my family life with David and our four children, and my identification with and passion for the growing global pro-life movement.

A POWERFUL
HISTORIC MOMENT

People may recall that *Roe v. Wade* was a Supreme Court decision, but few remember that this epic legal battle began in Dallas. Roe was Norma Lea Nelson McCorvey, a woman who illegally sought an abortion after finding she was pregnant for the third time. Two attorneys worked with McCorvey to challenge a Texas law that outlawed abortion. The court assigned her the name Roe because Doe, the first choice for an anonymous plaintiff, had been used in an earlier abortion case.

Wade was Henry Wade, the Dallas County district attorney who became famous for prosecuting Jack Ruby for killing Lee Harvey Oswald, who assassinated President John F. Kennedy. Wade defended the Texas law outlawing abortion, but he lost, and the law was declared unconstitutional. Following a series of appeals from both sides, the case wound its way to the Supreme Court for the famous 1973 ruling.

Roe v. Wade was originally filed in a district court in Dallas. As I shared my story at the 2020 North Texas March for Life, I stood at that very place. The actual courthouse in 1973 had been torn down and a new one erected, but the space I occupied was where history was made.

I had the feeling people sometimes have when they visit Gettysburg or some other historic battlefield. I felt powerfully connected to history. But that's not even the beginning of everything I was thinking about as I stood on those courthouse steps.

It was the same courthouse where I was legally adopted. The place where, at the sound of a judge's gavel, I was given a new name and a new family. And where a child nobody wanted became a child who was desperately wanted and deeply loved.

Mom and Dad carried me out of that courthouse and drove me to a nearby home where we were staying with our friends the Popes as my adoption process came to a close.

That was the home where I first met Tonya and her family.

Near the courthouse was the hospital where I was wheeled into an operating room, ready to undergo surgery for my dislocated hip.

Down the road a bit farther was the spot where my parents did something they had never done before and would never do again: they protested in front of an abortion clinic. I observed the proceedings from the comfort of my baby stroller.

Now, three decades later, there I was, telling my story to thousands of people. Talk about coming full circle!

Think about it for a minute.

I wasn't supposed to be alive, but I am.

I'm a chronic introvert, but I've spoken to millions of people through live events and the media.

I hardly knew or cared about the pro-life movement until I learned I had survived an abortion and I found myself living in a neighborhood that was a hotbed of pro-life activism.

I married a fellow adoptee, and today we're parenting our four kids.

I'm growing in my commitment to serving the pro-life movement as the movement itself grows more powerful—due in part to a president who is so committed to the movement that he became the first president to speak in person at the annual March for Life in Washington, DC. There he addressed a crowd of half a million people from the same stage where I stood and spoke an hour earlier.

Nobody could've made all this up! My life was an adventure even before it officially began. It remains an adventure today, and I wouldn't have it any other way.

This is not a story I would have ever imagined writing, but I like it just fine.

AFTERWORD

. . .

*D*OTTIE AND I HAVE KNOWN CLAIRE'S FAMILY FOR decades—long before they were her family! It's thrilling to see how her wonderful, complicated story has now come full circle.

I met Warren Culwell at Ole Miss, and he soon became my valued assistant. After Warren started dating Barbara and getting more and more serious about her, I gave him some advice: "Put a ring on it."

One of the best days in our lives was when Dottie and I adopted our wonderful daughter Heather. After Warren and Barbara found they could not give birth to their own children, Dottie and Barbara had plenty of opportunities to talk about the joys of adopting a child—a beautiful process that mirrors our adoption into Christ's family.

We cheered as they experienced the joys of the adoption process themselves, a process they documented in pictures, newsletters, and phone calls. They were walking a similar path to the one we had walked.

Their loving commitment to Christ and their years spent serving students through Campus Crusade—now called Cru—

uniquely prepared them to raise Claire and her sister, Rachel, in their faith.

Only later did we learn Claire's amazing story of surviving abortion, reuniting with her birth mother, and gradually becoming a powerful pro-life speaker and advocate/activist for life.

Claire has a calling to speak personally, passionately, and compassionately about life issues. She knows firsthand about abortion's deadly impact, but she shares a message of love and healing that can touch any person from any perspective.

She calls believers and churches to follow her loving, gracious approach to women and men who are struggling through unexpected or unwanted pregnancies.

It was years before Claire and her parents unraveled the mystery of her birth. Now that they know the full story, they've told it here in *Survivor*. It's a story of beauty, pain, regret, redemption, and encouragement.

I wholeheartedly recommend this book to anyone interested in abortion, adoption, and wonderful life stories that reveal the glory and wisdom of our creator.

> —Josh McDowell, founder,
> Josh McDowell Ministry,
> an outreach of Cru

ACKNOWLEDGMENTS

. . .

THERE ARE MANY PEOPLE I WANT TO THANK FOR THEIR roles in my life and this book.

God. Thank you for writing this story for my life and giving me a platform to share it. Your hope for the world is life changing. Your promises concerning who I am have never changed. I pray that I honor you through my story.

My parents, Warren and Barbara Culwell. You have been my biggest cheerleaders. I am thankful that God chose you to be my parents. You are the most godly, steadfast, and wise parents. Your example of love and dedication shaped me. I love you! Thank you for your support as I tell our story. Thank you for wanting me, choosing me, loving me. You are everything to me.

My birth mother, Tonya. You are beautiful inside and out. Your story has touched millions of lives and will continue to through this book. Thank you for your courage and for allowing me to share our story. I am forever grateful to you for giving me my family. In doing that, you gave me everything. I love you!

My husband, David. You are my better half. Thank you for supporting all that I do without a single complaint. I can't wait to see what God has in store for our family. I wouldn't want to do life with anyone other than you. Your servant's heart, your unwavering support of what I do, the way you cheer for your kids in all areas of their life, and your loyalty to your family are a testament to who you are . . . and I'm proud that you are ours.

My children. You are my sunshine every day and my motivation to better our world. The greatest blessing I will ever have is to be your mama. I love you more than life! Always remember whose you are, and don't ever hesitate to come home. Our home and our hearts will forever be yours, even when you grow up. Your dad and I are so proud of who you are.

My sister, Rachel. Being your big sister is one of the greatest joys of my life. I am so proud of you, and I love you. I will forever cherish the memories we share. Thank you for being my example of what it looks like to follow Jesus, love others well, and be bold in standing for truth. You may be my baby sister, but I will always be the one learning from you.

My brother-in-law, Andrew. I am thankful that you are a part of our family and for how you love Rachel. I am looking forward to the memories that will be made now that you are in our family.

My niece Charlotte. I wrote this book because I am fighting for your future, just like your cousins'. I love you, sweet girl!

Dennis, Maria, Travis, and Becky. Thank you for your support. I am thankful to be a part of your family, and I am especially thankful for the ways you have lifted us up and helped us during years and years of my travel. I know you could have never imagined that God would write your family's story with someone like me in it, but as we know, he always knows what is good and best. The beautiful adoption stories that we share in our family speak to the goodness of God, and I can't help but smile when I think about what he did when he brought our Culwell and Holley families together. I love each of you dearly!

My extended family of aunts, uncles, cousins. Your support and encouragement from the beginning have meant the world to me. Many of you have spoken words to me that still encourage me today. I am blessed to have been adopted into such an incredible family.

The Dodds family (aka my other family). Thank you for being such enthusiastic and encouraging cheerleaders. Your wisdom and encouragement throughout my life have helped shape me. I love each of you dearly.

Abby. Thank you for being a loyal friend during the past ten years. We have been through so many ups and downs together since both of our lives changed so drastically through our opposition to abortion. I cherish the memories we share and the bond we have. You have always supported me and lifted me up, and I am forever grateful to call you one of my most treasured friends.

Heather, Karen, Bobby, and Shawn at the Coalition for Life in Bryan–College Station. Thank you for believing in my story and taking the time to care for my soul like you did. Your fight for women and the unborn ignited a fire in my heart to use my story for good: for life. I am so glad that it was all of you out on the sidewalk that day after I met my birth mother, who told me about my survival. The four of you changed my life.

Jamie C. Since we were sixteen, you have been one of the best friends a girl could ask for. Thank you for being there for all the most significant moments in my life, for driving to College Station to hear me speak for the first time, and for helping me put my story down on paper so that others could read it. You helped me believe in myself!

Matt and Lori Fatheree and Bill and Brenda Swinney. Thank you for believing in the significance of my story and helping make it possible to share it with others.

My many girlfriends: Robyn M., Jamye J., Nichola M., Rachel G., Brittany G., Amy O., Carrie T., Heather G., Rachel D., Michelle D., Melissa O., Karen J., Kim J., Charlotte O., Daria M., Diane S., Renae S., Grace W., Nevada C., Reem C., Lisa B., and many others. Each of you has played a role in shaping the woman I am today. Thank you for traveling with me to my speaking events, encouraging me, giving me feedback, and being examples to me of what it looks like to run after truth and fight for justice and, most importantly, what it looks like to be a loyal friend. I admire each of you, and I am so thankful for your friendship.

Laura Ruth. I am so thankful for you. You have been such a light and encouragement in my life and in many big moments of sharing my story across the country. You make me laugh like nobody else, and your faithful prayers have been so appreciated. I struck gold in our friendship.

Gary and Jeannie. It is no accident that we became neighbors who grew to love each other like family. I'm thankful for your constant support, prayers, love for my family, care for my children, and friendship.

Gregory. Thank you for being the most joyful and encouraging person in my life. I'm thankful for you and the way you help me appreciate life.

Joe Pojman of the Texas Alliance for Life. Whenever I think of you, I think of something you always say to me: "Claire, that speech you gave is the best one I've ever heard you give." You certainly have the gift of encouragement. Not only have you been a voice of encouragement and truth in my life, but you have also tirelessly worked to stop injustice, speak truth, pass effective legislation, and support pro-life efforts across Texas and around the world. You are servant hearted, dedicated, and one of the hardest workers I know, and I am so incredibly thankful for your efforts. I am even more thankful to call you a friend.

Gary Groth. I will always remember the moment you walked into my parents' living room to film our story. You were the most joyful, caring, thoughtful, and encouraging filmmaker/producer I had worked with. You radiated Christ in your question asking, your pondering, your thoughtful responses, and your desire to make the person being interviewed feel valued and heard. I am so grateful that it was you who filmed my birth mother for the first time. You made her feel heard; you connected with her heart; you cared. You helped lift a weight off her shoulders that day in her living room as you filmed her side of our story. She looked at me after you filmed her story and said, "Claire, I feel free." You have that effect on people; you make people feel like they matter. Thank you for seeing, valuing, and loving people like you do.

Deaconess Pregnancy and Adoption of Oklahoma City and Debbie Campbell. Our journey started at Deaconess with you, and our reunion twenty-one years later did too. What a unique story to tell: the same person who stood by my birth mother's side reunited us twenty-one years later. I'm so thankful it was Debbie. I remember the day I called and found out that she had kept my baby picture on her desk for twenty-one years. What I know now is that she knew what a miracle God had worked to give me life. Debbie and everyone at Deaconess gave my birth mother the only hope she had during her weeks living there as a pregnant teenager. Thank you for the life-giving option of adoption that your ministry provides, and thank you for loving your birth mothers so well.

Christopher Schweickert. Thank you for valuing my birth mother's story enough to take the time to put it on paper with her. You used your gifts and abilities as an attorney to help her heal as she navigated the tough questions you asked her. With every answer, you delicately encouraged her, wept with her, and valued her. I could never say thank you enough for the way you allowed God to use you in our lives.

Evan. Thank you for believing in my story enough to constantly go above and beyond to help me pretend like I'm tech savvy. Your willingness to help me and your devotion to the pro-life cause at such a young age have been refreshing and a big part of the incredible reach and effectiveness of my story. Your part in it all is so important and appreciated. I'm thankful to call you a friend.

Fellow survivors that I have met on this journey. It has been an encouragement to know you and relate to you. I am thankful for your survival, your lives, and the fact that we find family in one another. I pray that this book is an encouragement to you in your journey of life and healing.

Wes Yoder, Gloria Leyda, and the Ambassador Speakers Bureau team. Thank you for seeing my story as one that needs to be shared with the world and for believing in my ability to share it from the beginning. The platform and encouragement you have given me have pushed me to reflect the redemption and forgiveness in my story while boldly speaking truth.

Lois and Steve Rabey. Thank you for using your gift to make this book come to life. Your way with words—your ability to relate to my story and put my experiences on paper—is amazing. I am thankful that God brought us together to tell my story.

Christy Decker. This book wouldn't have been possible without your help. Thank you for putting words to my story and helping me understand what my heart wanted to share. You are an incredible writer and friend. I am thankful for you.

WaterBrook publishing team. Thank you for believing in my story and wanting to publish it. Your hard work and dedication have been inspiring, and I am so thankful for all you've done.

Pastors John Hagee and Matt Hagee (Cornerstone Church and Sanctuary of Hope), Jim Daly (Focus on the Family), and Tony Perkins (Family Research Council). You are four men of God who have had an impact on my life through your leadership, your fight for life, and your thoughtfulness in relating to my story. Each of you expressed to me what every survivor longs to hear: "I see you, I hear you, I care, and I want to do something about it." Thank you for leading in such a God-honoring way.

Gayle Clark. Your love for Riley-Jane, the way you radiated joy about who she was, the way you spoke about her, and the way you cared for her ignited a fire in me. I want to be just like that with everyone I ever meet. Thank you for modeling love so well and for sharing Riley-Jane with me. I learned more about Jesus through you and Riley-Jane than I ever had before, and I knew I wanted to run after him. Thank you for giving me a glimpse of heaven in my time with RJ.

My birth mother's family: Bryan, Whitney, Alex, and Payton. I am so grateful to know you and to have been welcomed into your family. I celebrate the life that God gave each of you!

Presley Ace. In the short time I knew you, I saw the hand of God on your life. You were perfectly created in the image of God. Whitney, thank you for including me in her life. She affected me in ways that words cannot express.

And to my grandparents who are no longer with us: Grand-daddy, GranFran, MamaPeach, Doc, Grammy, and Gramps. I so wish you could be here now to witness what God is doing through our family's story. I am thankful for the impact on my life that each of you had that is evident in my life and my story today. I have always known that I was wanted and that I belonged because of your love. When I picture heaven, I picture all of you loving on my twin.

GOING FURTHER

. . .

THANK YOU FOR READING MY STORY. NOW YOU MAY BE asking yourself questions like these:

How can I help?

Can God use me even if I don't have a story to tell?

What are next steps I can take?

Great! God will use you if you allow him to.

Each one of us has our own connections, resources, talents, gifts, abilities, communities, and personalities that he can use. We just need to be willing!

GOING DEEPER

There are many ways you can get involved in the pro-life movement.

Pray

Every one of us can do this.

Pray for an end to abortion.

Pray for changed hearts among women facing unplanned pregnancies.

Pray for conversion of souls.

Pray that people will embrace adoption and love children who are not wanted.

Pray for the healing of post-abortive men and women
who struggle with guilt and fear.

Pray for God to give you the words to start conversations about respecting life in your home, your community, your congregation.

Talk

Start the conversation about life with your children, your friends,
your pastor.

Get Involved

Pro-life ministries in your area need your help. You can support
them financially, donate items, offer your time and your gifts,
or talk about their services in your community so that everyone knows they are there. Please support them in any way you
can.

Vote

Make sure your political decisions reflect your beliefs and values.
Do your research; then take the time to vote for the candidate
that values all life, born and unborn. If we Americans can't pre-

serve the right to life, how can we fight against any other injustice?

Share

Talk about real-life stories of people who have been affected by abortion, adoption, and life.

ORGANIZATIONS YOU
CAN SUPPORT

I recommend that you start by getting involved in organizations in your own community.

I also want to recommend that you support these organizations that are serving women and families and providing great resources.

40 Days for Life

This group, which was born in the College Station neighborhood where I lived, is now an international group that organizes campaigns against abortion in more than sixty nations.

www.40daysforlife.com

Sanctuary of Hope

At a time when many believers turn their backs on women facing unplanned pregnancies, Cornerstone Church's ministry to pregnant mothers embraces them and their children.

www.jhm.org/sohcares

Deaconess Pregnancy & Adoption

This is the wonderful agency that helped Tonya when she was pregnant with me and then found my adoptive parents. Organizations like this need your support.

    https://deaconessadoption.org

And Then There Were None

This ministry helps people like my dear friend Abby Johnson, abortion clinic workers who want to leave the abortion industry.

    https://abortionworker.com

Live Action

Founded by fifteen-year-old Lila Rose, this organization specializes in undercover videos that expose the underside of the abortion industry, including Planned Parenthood clinics.

    www.liveaction.org

The Radiance Foundation

This group spreads the message that many people need to hear: every human life has purpose.

    www.theradiancefoundation.org

Embrace Grace

More than six thousand single moms and women facing unplanned pregnancies have participated in this ministry's network of church-based support groups.

    https://embracegrace.com

The Abortion Survivors Network

I'm not the only one! This organization provides networking, community, and support for those of us who have survived abortions.
  https://abortionsurvivors.org

Surrendering the Secret

Many women who have experienced abortion hide the secret of abortion deep in their hearts, suffering feelings of shame, failure, and guilt in isolation. This group connects women through study groups led by volunteers throughout the nation and beyond.
  www.surrenderingthesecret.com

NOTES

· · ·

CHAPTER 1: CHOSEN, LOVED, ADOPTED

1. Kathleen Silber and Phylis Speedlin, *Dear Birth Mother: Thank You for Our Baby*, 2nd ed. (San Antonio: Corona, 1991).

CHAPTER 7: THE UNRAVELING

1. "Born-Alive Abortion Survivors: Documented Cases," Susan B. Anthony List, www.sba-list.org/born-alive-abortion-survivors-documented -cases; "Claire Culwell: Abortion Survivor," Susan B. Anthony List, August 31, 2019, www.sba-list.org/newsroom/claire-culwell-abortion -survivor.

CHAPTER 8: MY YEAR OF DESTINY

1. See "About," Coalition for Life, https://coalitionforlife.com /about-us and Sarah Pulliam Bailey, "Planned Parenthood Puts Restraining Order on Former Director," *Christianity Today*, November 4, 2009, www .christianitytoday.com/women/2009/november/planned-parenthood-puts -restraining-order-on-former.html.

2. The HBO documentary *Soldiers in the Army of God* covered some of these activists, directed by Marc Levin and Daphne Pinkerson (New York: Off Line Entertainment Group, 2000).

3. "Abortion Doctor Slain Inside Kansas Church," *Seattle Times*, June 1, 2009, www.seattletimes.com/nation-world/abortion-doctor-slain-inside-kansas-church; Roxana Hegeman, "Man Who Killed Abortion Doctor Gets More Lenient Sentence," AP, November 23, 2016, https://apnews.com/24 fcd54bbf054d75b3d56aa48e391852.

4. Daniel Victor and Jack Healy, "Garrett Swasey, Officer Killed in Colorado, Is Recalled for Courage and Faith," *New York Times*, November 28, 2015, www.nytimes.com/2015/11/28/us/garrett-swasey-officer-killed-in-colorado-is-recalled-for-courage-and-faith.html.

5. Auditi Guha, "In Alabama, an Anti-Choice Protester Tried to Run Over an Abortion Clinic Escort," Rewire News Group, May 8, 2019, https://rewire.news/article/2019/05/08/in-alabama-an-anti-choice-protester-tried-to-run-over-an-abortion-clinic-escort.

CHAPTER 9: MY STORY, MY CALLING

1. Jessica Shaver Renshaw, *Gianna: Aborted, and Lived to Tell About It* (Carol Stream, IL: Tyndale, 2011); *October Baby*, directed by Jon Erwin and Andrew Erwin (Franklin, TN: Provident Films, 2011).

2. Lindsey Bever, "The Only Reason I Am Alive Is the Fact That the Abortionist Had Not Yet Arrived at Work," *Washington Post*, September 30, 2016, www.washingtonpost.com/news/acts-of-faith/wp/2016/09/27/the-only-reason-i-am-alive-is-the-fact-that-the-abortionist-had-not-yet-arrived-at-work.

3. Cheryl Wetzstein, "Planned Parenthood Misleads, Women Testify at Congressional Hearing," *Washington Times*, September 9, 2015, www.washingtontimes.com/news/2015/sep/9/planned-parenthood-misleads-women-testify-congress.

4. "About Live Action," Live Action, www.liveaction.org.

5. Kate Shellnutt, "33 Under 33," *Christianity Today*, July 1, 2014, www.christianitytoday.com/ct/2014/july-august/33-under-33.html?share=a20r wfl%2fZxLPmGUtmUPHyhTYGEXyclWH.

6. "Joe Pojman, Ph.D.," Texas Alliance for Life, www.texasallianceforlife.org/joe-pojman.

7. "Planned Parenthood Facility Repurposed in Bryan, Texas," *CCM Magazine*, October 29, 2015, www.ccmmagazine.com/news/planned-parenthood-facility-repurposed-in-bryan-texas.

8.   Leah Hickman, "Buildings with Baggage: Groups Are Turning Old Abortion Centers into Pro-Life Spaces, but the Facilities' Horrific Histories Are Difficult for Many to Overcome," *World*, January 2, 2020, https://world.wng.org/2020/01/buildings_with_baggage.

CHAPTER 11: TURNING ASHES INTO BEAUTY

1.   "The Men Who Feel Left Out of US Abortion Debate," BBC, August 28, 2019, www.bbc.com/news/world-us-canada-49240582.

2.   "Adoption Statistics," Adoption History Project, https://pages.uoregon.edu/adoption/topics/adoptionstatistics.htm.

3.   Lisa Cannon Green, "Survey: Women Go Silently From Church to Abortion Clinic," June 21, 2018, www.focusonthefamily.com/pro-life/survey-women-go-silently-from-church-to-abortion-clinic.

4.   Green, "Survey."

5.   "Study of Women Who Have Had an Abortion and Their Views on Church," copyright © 2016 Care Net, www.care-net.org/hubfs/Downloads/CareNet-research_abortion-in-church.pdf.

6.   Jenna Jerman, Rachel K. Jones, and Tsuyoshi Onda, "Characteristics of U.S. Abortion Patients in 2014 and Changes Since 2008," Guttmacher Institute, May 2016, www.guttmacher.org/report/characteristics-us-abortion-patients-2014.

7.   John Hagee, "The Vision Becomes Reality!" Hagee Ministries, www.jhm.org/sohcares.

8.   "Young*Lives*—Teen Parents," Young Life, www.younglife.org/ForEveryKid/YoungLives/Pages/default.aspx; "Young Life History and Vision for the Future," Young Life, www.younglife.org/About/Pages/History.aspx.

9.   Embrace Grace Inc., https://embracegrace.com/our-story and https://embracegrace.com.

CHAPTER 12: EXPERIENCING GOD'S GRACE
AND REDEMPTION

1.   David Brody, "Brody File Exclusive: Donald Trump Explains Pro-Life Conversion," April 8, 2011, www1.cbn.com/thebrodyfile/archive

/2011/04/08/brody-file-exclusive-donald-trump-explains-pro-life
-conversion.

2.   Melissa Ohden, *You Carried Me: A Daughter's Memoir* (Walden, NY: Plough, 2017).

3.   Jim Daly, "Times Square Billboard Owners Are Refusing to Lease Us Space—Please Express Your Disappointment," Focus on the Family, May 1, 2019, https://jimdaly.focusonthefamily.com/times-square-billboard -owners-are-refusing-to-lease-us-space-please-express-your-disappointment.

4.   Kevin McCullough, "ALIVE from New York: The Day Abortion Died," Townhall, May 5, 2019, https://townhall.com/columnists/kevin mccullough/2019/05/05/alive-from-new-york-the-day-abortion-died -n2545863.

CLAIRE CULWELL speaks around the world about her unique life story and has been featured on *Focus on the Family* and many other news outlets. She lives in Austin, Texas, with her husband and their four children.

For information about Claire's speaking ministry, please contact Gloria Leyda at Ambassador Speakers Bureau:

www.ambassadorspeakers.com

info@ambassadorspeakers.com

615-370-4700

Claire would love to connect with you. You can follow her via social media:

www.claireculwell.com

@claireculwell

This book was set in Fournier, a typeface named for Pierre-Simon Fournier (1712–68), the youngest son of a French printing family. He started out engraving wood-blocks and large capitals, then moved on to fonts of type. In 1736 he began his own foundry and made several important contributions in the field of type design; he is said to have cut 147 alphabets of his own creation. Fournier is probably best remembered as the designer of St. Augustine Ordinaire, a face that served as the model for the Monotype Corporation's Fournier, which was released in 1925.